Numeracy and Accounting

Numeracy and Accounting

G Blake and T Daff

Pitman

PITMAN PUBLISHING LIMITED
39 Parker Street, London WC2B 5PB

Associated Companies
Copp Clark Pitman, Toronto/Fearon Pitman Publishers Inc, San Francisco/
Pitman Publishing New Zealand Ltd, Wellington/Pitman Publishing Pty
Ltd, Melbourne

© G Blake and T Daff 1979

First published in Great Britain 1979

Text set in 11 on 13pt Times at George Over Limited, London and Rugby.
Printed by photolithography and bound in Great Britain
at The Pitman Press, Bath

ISBN 0 273 01323 8

Contents

Acknowledgements

We are deeply indebted to Margaret French-Greenslade as typist, to her husband Nigel for proof reading and to Rosemary Westley for typing the accounts.

Our thanks go to Jim Deans (one time HM Inspector and BEC Officer) and Margaret Berriman of Pitman for their help and guidance. Our thanks also to the Business Education Council for permission to reproduce Module 2 National Level Objectives, and to the Banking Education Service.

We are also grateful to the following organisations for allowing us to reproduce data and diagrams from their annual reports:

Associated Television Corporation Ltd

The Bowater Corporation Ltd

Chrysler United Kingdom Ltd

The Electricity Council

The Ladbroke Group Ltd

The Legal and General Assurance Society Ltd

The Midland Educational Co Ltd

United Biscuits (Holdings) Ltd

and to HW Peel and Company Ltd for permission to reproduce an example of their semi-logarithmic graph paper; to AMG Law, Chief chemist of Carbonum Ltd for information on the development of carbon papers; to RD Parham, Director of Finance, Chrysler United Kingdom Ltd for assistance with Assignment 5.

Finally, this book could not have been finished without the support and patience of our wives.

Preface

The authors believe that in writing a textbook to meet the objectives of BEC National Level Module 2 it is implicit upon them to take note of the BEC philosophy. This seems to them expressed most clearly in the central themes of Money, People, Communication and a Logical and Numerate approach to business problems. Writing a Numeracy and Accounting textbook makes it easy to cover two of these themes. Nevertheless, the People and Communication aspects are important. To act as a reminder that the skills of numeracy and accounting are concerned with people, the book is set in one company, thus providing an opportunity to follow progress over a period of time. The exercises and assignments will test the mind of the student to ensure not only that skills are being acquired but also that those skills can be communicated to others.

For many students, this module will be their only contact with accounts at National Level, so there is a need to ensure that they understand *why* certain things are done. For the remaining students it will provide a foundation for further study in accounts, so they need to know *how* to do the required accounting transactions. To meet these two objectives, exercises are included for both types of student, and teaching staff may select whichever exercises are appropriate.

BEC National Level objectives for Module 2 are included in the book and reference is made to them throughout. The inclusion of the objectives should not encourage the reader to carry out a ticking operation, however, as it is quite possible that the objectives will be interpreted in different ways.

The integration of numeracy and accounting breaks new ground and the authors'decision as to the most logical approach to teach this module may not meet with everyone's approval. It is based upon the premise that it is the purpose of the module to convey a clear understanding of basic accounts and basic numeracy. The authors have used the accounts to provide the logic for the sequencing of the subject matter and have integrated the numeracy appropriately.

By integrating the numeracy at appropriate points, the authors recognise that there may well be some conflict and repetition for students doing the Applied Statistics Option Module. The conflict can be resolved by close co-operation with the Applied Statistics lecturer and the repetition should be seen as an opportunity to restate and reinforce objectives. Certain aspects of numeracy will appear in different modules which will provide an opportunity to see another application for a particular technique. The inclusion of numeracy in this module was not solely for the purpose of showing its use in accounting, but to act as a basis for application across the whole field of business activity, and exercises which draw upon differing business situations have been included.

The authors have deliberately omitted certain aspects of a more usual accounting course at this level to make the students' learning load manageable. The omissions include petty cash, control accounts, incomplete records, income and expenditure accounts, manufacturing and partnership accounts.

The textual matter will provide adequate instruction, but questions at the end of the unit require the student to do more than just repeat certain steps, so new information will have to be sought, for example, from the library.

Four appendices allow those lecturers who have the time, to extend the students' study, but if this time is not available, omission of the appendices will not affect the ability of the student to complete the course.

Realistic figures have been used throughout, including actual company figures. This means that some of the calculations are not convenient round numbers, but it is expected that students will have calculators available to be used as and when the lecturer considers it appropriate.

A series of assignments have been interleaved after the units which provide the necessary input of knowledge. Assignment 5 has been inserted before the last unit so that students can be completing this before the end of the course, and can hand it in on completion of the last unit. For this reason, the last unit includes a lot of matter which could well have been included in Unit 1, but because of the practical reasons of completing assignments as assessment of the course, it seemed preferable to hold this material until the end and use it as a base for placing accounts in the context of the overall progression of technology.

Business Education Council National Awards

Common Core Module 2:
Numeracy and Accounting

1 Aims

1.1   help establish and develop basic numerical skills so that the student can use these to derive full benefit from the course as a whole

1.2   assist the student to understand the function of accounting in business, through a study of its basic concepts and methods

1.3   provide a basis for subsequent studies in accountancy, either within the course, or later in the student's career

1.4   enable the student to apply numerical and accounting skills and understanding to business problems, in a way which will increase his/her immediate and future effectiveness in employment.

2   General Objectives

On completion of this book the student should be able to:

A   carry out arithmetical calculations and basic algebraic operations

B   construct and interpret graphs involving the accurate plotting of data and simple functions

C   represent and interpret data in tabular and diagrammatic form

D   calculate and interpret selected indices and measures of central tendency

E   outline the development and purpose of accounting

F   describe and explain accounting concepts and conventions

G   record financial information and prepare financial statements in accordance with accounting concepts

H interpret accounting information
J use the skills and concepts acquired to assist in the evaluation of simple business problems.

3 Learning Objectives

In the course of work on this book and, as appropriate, in other course work, the student should be able to:

Book
Unit
Reference

A Carry out arithmetical calculations and basic algebraic operations

A.1	add, subtract, multiply and divide integers, decimals and fractions	1
A.2	convert fractions to decimals and vice versa	1
A.3	calculate percentages and ratios from given information	1
A.4	calculate and manipulate roots and powers	App. B
A.5	solve simple equations	2

B Construct and interpret graphs involving the accurate plotting of data and simple functions

B.1	distinguish between discrete and continuous data and between dependent and independent variables	7
B.2	plot scatter diagrams	7
B.3	draw graphs of simple functions	7
B.4	interpret the natural and semi-log scale graph	7

G Record financial information and prepare financial statements in accordance with accounting concepts

G.1 outline and illustrate the way in which accounting entries are linked to business activity through data collection   All

G.2 classify, record and summarise business transactions in appropriate accounting books and records, and extract therefrom a Trial Balance   2, 3, 4, 10, 11, 13

G.3 identify and record the adjustments necessary to compile simple Profit and Loss Accounts and Balance Sheets   6, 7, 14, 15

G.4 prepare simple Profit and Loss Accounts and Balance Sheets in appropriate form   6, 7, 9

H Interpret accounting information

H.1 calculate and explain the significance and limitations of basic financial ratios from given data   16

J Use the skills and concepts acquired to assist in the evaluation of simple business problems

J.1 select and apply the numerical methods to the analysis of a given business problem   Assignment 5

J.2 select and apply the appropriate accounting concepts and methods to business situations including those not previously encountered   Assignment 4

J.3 analyse and evaluate a simple business problem requiring the use of both numerical and accounting abilities   Assignment 4

J.4 employ selected numerical and accounting abilities to describe, analyse and evaluate simple business problems incorporating knowledge and skills developed in other modules.   Assignment 5

1 Introduction

In the United Kingdom there are few restrictions upon the setting up of a business. Generally speaking, anyone is free to establish his own business, although there are laws which govern various aspects of business life.

Before a person can begin a business he must possess **capital**. Capital represents the money or goods which the proprietor invests in his business. The amount of capital needed to establish a business in a given field of activity depends largely upon the type of business. There are no laws establishing a minimum amount of capital needed.

Thus, if you wish to begin a window cleaning business the only equipment needed would be a bucket, a leather, an extension ladder and a bicycle. In all, you would probably purchase these for a total of about £100.

On the other hand, if you wished to go into business as a garage owner, you would necessarily require a greater capital to purchase the land and buildings, the specialist equipment and the stocks of petrol, oil and accessories.

Most people who start up their own business use their own savings or money borrowed from the family. Whilst banks will lend some money to help a business to start, they will only lend a proportion of the necessary capital, they will not put up all of the money required. For this reason businesses owned by a single person tend to be rather small. They are limited by the amount of capital available to the owner.

The purpose of any business is to earn profits. The businessman may do this by trading — that is buying and selling — by manufacturing items from raw materials or by selling services as do insurance companies, banks, and so on.

Marks and Spencer is primarily a trading concern. The Ford Motor Company is primarily a manufacturing concern. Barclays sells banking services. Each firm seeks to earn profits for its owners.

Firms generate profits by purchasing **factors of production** i.e. buying equipment, hiring labour, purchasing raw materials and by selling the resulting product or service for a price greater than its cost.

In business it is the entrepreneur, the person who finances and controls the undertaking, who decides what products or services to provide and how and when to provide them. He backs his judgment with his capital. If his judgment is sound and his products sell, then he recoups the profit. If his judgment is faulty, he must stand the losses. In return for undertaking the risks associated with business ventures, he is entitled to the profits of his success.

While the entrepreneur retains sole ownership of the business he is referred to as a **sole trader**. He may employ a number of people; the word sole refers to ownership not to employees. There are certain advantages to being in sole ownership of a business, for example, independence in action, direct responsibility, reaping the rewards of a profitable business. There are also disadvantages, for example, the owner may lack sufficient money to expand the business and this may cause him to look around for a partner, someone willing to invest money in the business and/or additional help in running the organisation. The partnership organisation offers certain advantages already mentioned, but the major disadvantage for both the sole trader and the partnership is that if the organisation meets hard times and losses are made, the owner(s) is liable for the losses from his personal possessions and wealth − referred to as unlimited liability.

This disadvantage is resolved by making the organisation a **limited company** so that any losses incurred are the company's losses and not those of the people running the business. The owners buy shares in the limited company and the maximum extent of their loss is the purchase price of the shares. There are legal implications in becoming a limited company which bring certain accounting responsibilities, but in a basic accounting text it is unnecessary to become involved with these. The principles are best understood by considering the accounting procedures of a sole trader. The organisation used in this textbook is Numac Trading Company started by C Brown (as a sole trader) in January 195–. It is a general trading company involved in buying and selling goods and so is not involved in manufacturing items. This text, therefore, will not be concerned with producing the specialised manufacturing accounts required by such firms.

A businessman needs information to assist him in his decision-making e.g. what to buy, when to sell, how to sell, at what price, what to make, how to make it, who to sell it to. Some of this will be produced outside his business by government agencies, trade associations and chambers of commerce. Other information will be generated within his own business.

This mass of facts and figures — whether produced within the business or outside — is generally referred to as **data**. Data are unstructured, unrelated facts and figures. Before a businessman can use these facts and figures he must arrange them so as to reveal certain relationships and highlight important features. This is done in a number of ways, by pictorial representation (graphs and charts), by tabulation (putting figures into a table) or through some other method of presentation. Only when raw data has been processed in this way does it become meaningful to the businessman; only then does it, in fact, become **information**. Once data has been converted into information, the businessman can usefully employ it as a guide to making decisions.

Data is transformed into information through **systems**. A system selects and processes data in order that it can become meaningful to the business. Thus, the fact that in any one summer more red cotton dresses are being sold than of any other colour will only be important information for a dress company; it will be of little interest to a fishmonger. The dress company will therefore design a system for itself, to monitor fashion changes. The firm's management will base decisions about the nature of future products — their design, colour etc — upon the information produced by the system.

A firm will institute numerous systems in its attempt to make sense of the data flowing into it. One of the more important systems is a firm's accounting system. The accounting record will enable the business to control income and expenditure, to gauge the pattern of sales, and to assess the profitability of various activities.

The task of simply recording business transactions is known as **book-keeping**. It is essential that accurate and up-to-date records are maintained, otherwise decisions will be based on faulty information. The analysis of book-keeping information and its use in decision-making comes under the heading of accounting and finance, but before one can manipulate accounting information, the nature and limitations of the recording process must be thoroughly understood. It is this basic understanding that this book aims to provide.

Accounting information may be presented in formal accounting statements or in tabular or pictorial form. Note, too, that the firm's accounts are only one source of information; there are many others.

Organisations in the retail business are daily involved in exercises on pricing. A retailer knows the price he has paid for an item and has to decide upon its selling price. The difference between the purchase price and the selling price is called **mark-up**. Prices do not always remain the same; during sale time prices may be lowered. It is important for whoever is calculating price increases or decreases to be able to calculate a percentage. Generally, prices of similar articles have the same percentage increase or decrease.

Assume that our organisation, Numac Trading Company, sells shoes which have a unit purchase price of £7.50 and a mark up of 30%. To work out the selling price it is only necessary to multiply £7.50 by $^{30}/_{100}$ (to find 30%) giving £2.25. Adding this £2.25 to the £7.50 gives us a selling price of £9.75.

Do recognise that £7.50 + 30% is not the same as £9.75 − 30%. Calculate it for yourself. It is not the same because 30% is being calculated on two different figures i.e. £7.50 and £9.75, so they cannot possibly give the same answer. Nevertheless, it is a trap many people fall into.

To calculate a percentage increase use the following procedure:

$$\frac{\text{New Figure} - \text{Old Figure}}{\text{Old Figure}} \times 100 = \text{Percentage Change}$$

or Percentage Change × Old Figure = New Figure − Old Figure
(actual change)

Using the above figures as an example, the percentage increase in the price of shoes is:

$$\frac{9.75 - 7.50}{7.50} \times 100 = \frac{2.25}{7.50} \times 100 = 30\%$$

Thus $\dfrac{30}{100} \times 7.50 = £2.25$

It is quite likely that at some time there will be a need to determine a percentage increase or decrease from a change in absolute numbers. For example, using the price of £9.75 for shoes, Numac Trading Company may wish to sell these shoes at £8.95 because the new selling price has a certain selling attraction. Nevertheless, the Sales Manager may wish to know what the percentage drop is. The calculation is as follows:

$$\frac{\text{New Figure} - \text{Old Figure}}{\text{Old Figure}} \times 100 = \text{Percentage Change}$$

$$\frac{8.95 - 9.75}{9.75} \times 100 = \frac{-0.80}{9.75} \times 100 = -8.20512\%$$

Thus the selling price has been reduced by 8.2%. (This is correct to one place of decimals).

The reader will notice that the figure of 8.20512 has been rounded to 8.2. Rounding of figures can be to the nearest whole number (called an integer) or to a certain number of decimal places. Rounding is done by looking at the next figure to the right of the required accuracy and if it is a 5 or more, increasing the figure to the left by 1. If it is a 4 or less, do not alter the figure to the left. The figure 8.20512 could be rounded in a number of ways:

a   to the nearest whole number (the next figure to the right is a 2 so do not alter 8). Answer 8
b   to the nearest one place of decimals (the next figure to the right is a 0 so do not alter 2). Answer 8.2
c   to the nearest two places of decimals (the next figure to the right is a 5 so add 1 to the 0). Answer 8.21
d   to the nearest three places of decimals (the next figure to the right is a 1 so do not alter 5). Answer 8.205

Developing these ideas a little further, assume that a product priced at £7.50 is to have its selling price reduced by $12^{1}/_{2}\%$. This can be achieved in a number of ways:

1   Multiply £7.50 $\times \dfrac{12^{1}/_{2}}{100}$ = £7.50 $\times \dfrac{25}{200}$ = £0.9375

When £0.9375 is rounded to the nearest penny, the final figure is £0.94, since the third figure is a 7. Subtract £0.94 from £7.50 to give £6.56.

2 Multiply $£7.50 \times \dfrac{100 - 12^1/_2}{100} = £7.50 \times \dfrac{87^1/_2}{100} = £6.5625$

When rounded to the nearest penny this becomes £6.56.

3 It might be recognised that $12^1/_2\%$ is equal to $^1/_8$ i.e. $\dfrac{12^1/_2}{100}$

Thus $\dfrac{£7.50}{8} = £0.9375$. When rounded to the nearest penny and subtracted from £7.50, the answer is £6.56.

4 A reduction of $^1/_8$th will leave $^7/_8$ths, so multiply £7.50 by $^7/_8$ to give £6.5625 and round to the nearest penny to give £6.56.

The advantage of **4** is that it is an easier calculation to perform without a calculator, and with a calculator it requires less keys to be pressed than the other three methods. It is therefore useful to learn the more common fractions with their respective percentage values.

Conversely, where a fraction needs to be converted to a percentage, multiply the fraction by 100 e.g.

$^1/_4$ converted to a % is $^1/_4 \times 100 = 25\%$
$^1/_3$ converted to a % is $^1/_3 \times 100 = 33^1/_3\%$

Note that it is better to use the fraction rather than the decimal where there is a recurring figure(s) i.e. $33^1/_3\%$ is preferable to 33.3333.

The conversion of decimals to fractions or percentages follows similar lines. What, for example, is meant by 0.3? The first figure to the right of the decimal point shows 10ths of the whole, the second figure 100ths and so on, thus 0.3 simply means $^3/_{10}$ and 0.35, $^{35}/_{100}$. If a decimal figure is to be expressed as a percentage, the decimal value must be multiplied by 100, thus $0.35 \times 100 = 35\%$. Take care: 0.3 is 30% (not 3%); 0.03 is 3%.

If you understand the above calculations there is a short cut when dealing with percentages, if all that is required is a new selling price without any need to know what the actual amount of the increase or decrease is. Numac Trading Company may wish to increase the price of shoes by 30%. 100 is taken to be the usual selling price of the goods, so this is added to the percentage increase. Thus, the 30% increase becomes 130% of the usual selling price. The usual selling price or starting figure (often referred to as the base figure) is then multiplied by this new figure to obtain the new, increased, selling price. For example, if a pair of shoes has a purchase price of £7.50 and a mark-up of 30%, the new selling price will be:

$$£7.50 \times \frac{130}{100} = £9.75$$

Sometimes a business may wish to reduce the price of its goods. For example, Numac Trading Company may wish to reduce the price of its cotton sheets by $12\frac{1}{2}\%$. 100 is again taken to be the usual selling price, so a $12\frac{1}{2}\%$ reduction will be $100 - 12\frac{1}{2}\%$ i.e. $87\frac{1}{2}\%$ of the usual selling price. If the usual selling price is £16.12, then the new, reduced, selling price will be:

$$£16.12 \times \frac{87\frac{1}{2}}{100} = £14.10\frac{1}{2}$$

Ratio

NUMAC TRADING CO

Sales (£)

Department	19-0	19-1
Textiles	160 000	160 000
Clothing	174 000	218 820
Furniture	150 000	261 580
Miscellaneous	89 000	89 000
Total	573 000	729 400

Above is a breakdown of the sales for Numac Trading Co over two years. Sometimes figures are too big to handle so it is acceptable to round the figures to the nearest £000 (thousand £). The table would then be as shown over the page.

```
┌────────────────────────────────────────────────┐
│               NUMAC TRADING CO                   │
│                                                  │
│              Sales (£000)                        │
│                                                  │
│   Department              19-0          19-1     │
│   Textiles                 160           160     │
│   Clothing                 174           219     │
│   Furniture                150           262     │
│   Miscellaneous             89            89     │
│   Total                    573           729     │
│                                                  │
└────────────────────────────────────────────────┘
```

Notice that the total for 19−1 is not the sum of the rounded figures. This is the way it should be shown when the original precise data is known. Where the original data is not known it would be permissible to add the figures given.

A statement can be made that the ratio of sales for 19−0 for Textiles to Clothing is 160 to 174. It does not matter if this is expressed as 160 000 to 174 000 or 160 to 174; the ratio is the same. A **ratio** shows a relationship between two or more variables.

Note that if the figures are increased by the same *proportion* (i.e. if they are multiplied or divided by the same amount) the ratio remains unchanged. So the ratio 160 to 174 is the same as 160 000 to 174 000. However, if the same amount is added to or subtracted from the figures, the ratio will change. Thus, if 30 is added to 160 and 174, the resulting ratio will be 190 to 204, which is entirely different from the ratio 160 to 174.

Thus, if ratio figures are *multiplied* or *divided* by the same value, the ratio is *unchanged*. If the same value is added to or subtracted from ratio figures, the ratio will be altered.

A start has been made in handling numerical data, and throughout this book further assistance will be given to assemble data and present it in a way which will assist understanding and management decision-making.

Summary

On completion of this unit plus practice at the exercises you should be able to:

1 Understand the meaning of the word 'business'.
2 Add, subtract, multiply and divide integers, decimals and fractions. (A1)
3 Convert fractions to decimals and vice versa. (A2)
4 Calculate percentages and ratios from given information. (A3)
5 Solve simple equations (A5)

(N.B. The alpha numeric code given in brackets refers to the Business Education Council National Awards Module 2 Learning Objectives, details of which are given at the front of this book.)

Exercises

1 Explain the meaning of the following:
data   book-keeping
systems   accounting
information

2 Collect six advertisements for accountants. Use these advertisements to describe the sort of job accountants are required to do, the type of industry they work in and the age and qualifications required.

3 Assume that the following stock record constitutes the total stock of Numac Trading Company. Calculate the value of stock at purchase price, then calculate the value of stock at selling price and determine gross profit (gross profit = sales − purchasing cost).

Description	Qty	Purchase price	Mark-up
Shoes, men	12	£7.50	30%
Towel, bath	55	£5.80	60%
Tights, one size	650	£0.40	15%
Sheets, cotton single	30	£12.40	30%
Sheets, cotton double	18	£17.30	30%

(Objective A3, J3)

4   In the stock list in Question 3 the mark-up percentages are different. What factors would cause a company to have a different mark-up figure for different products? Discuss the advantages in having the same mark-up figure for all the stock. (Objective J4)

5   A sentence in this unit states 'in return for undertaking the risks associated with business ventures, he (the entrepreneur) is entitled to the profits of his success'. Do you agree or disagree with this statement? Give your reasons. Are there any disadvantages of using profit as a sign of success or failure? (Towards Objective J2)

6   The value of stock (at its purchase price) of XYZ Ltd at the end of January 19−8 is £50 000. A fire on the night of 31 January 19−8 destroyed $^{1}/_{8}$ of the stock.
a   Calculate the value at purchase price of goods destroyed.
b   If the constant mark-up is 44%, calculate the value of sales lost.
c   Since gross profit is sales price less purchase cost, calculate the gross profit lost as a result of the fire.
d   The sales for 19−8 were £545 000. Calculate the sales lost as a percentage of the year's sales. (Objective A3)

7   Numac Trading Company has had in stock for some time 30 pairs of single cotton sheets purchased at £12.40 a pair. A local hotel has asked for a quotation for a supply of single cotton sheets. Numac makes the following offer:

Purchase of 10 pairs, selling price £12.00 per pair
Purchase of 20 pairs, selling price £11.75 per pair
Purchase of 30 pairs, selling price £11.50 per pair

a   Determine the actual loss involved and the percentage loss for each offer.
b· Why should any organisation consider selling any article at a loss? (Objective A3, J3)

8   In a simple interest calculation,

$$\text{Interest} = \frac{\text{Principal} \times \text{Rate} \times \text{Time (Years)}}{100} \quad \text{or} \quad I = \frac{P \times R \times T}{100}$$

N.B. Principal is the original sum of money on which interest is paid. If the interest is £8, the rate of interest (3%) and the time 15 months, calculate the principal. (Objectives A1, A5)

9   To calculate the return or yield on an investment in shares, the formula is:

$$\text{Yield} = \frac{\text{Income per share}}{\text{Cost per share}} \times 100$$

If the yield is $6^1/_4\%$ and the income 8p per share, how much did each share cost? (Objectives A1, A5)

10   The yield on shares is given by the above formula. In this case the income will be declared as a dividend on a share's nominal value. The relationship between income, dividend and nominal value is

$$\text{Income} = \frac{\text{Dividend}}{100} \times \text{Share Nominal Value}$$

Calculate the yield if a man buys shares at 40p with a nominal value of 10p, and a dividend of 17% is declared. (Objectives A1, A5)

11   A local authority raises its income by means of rates. All the premises within the local authority's district will be given a rateable value so that the district will have a total rateable value. The income required by the district council will be expressed as a proportion of the rateable value of each property. It can be expressed as

Income = Number of £'s rateable value × Rate.

If a district council has rateable property of £27 000 000 and the rate levied is 98p per £ of rateable value, calculate the income available to the district council. (Objectives A1, A5)

12   Using information provided in Question 11, another district council declares a rate of 78p per £ of rateable value and finds it has an income of £23 541 000. Calculate the rateable value of this district council. (Objectives A1, A5)

2 A simple accounting system — the Balance Sheet

Having considered the nature and purpose of a business, having been introduced to the idea of ordering data and having been told that one of the most important systems employed by a business is its accounting system, it is necessary now to examine that system in more detail. We will begin with an examination of the Balance Sheet.

The purpose of a Balance Sheet is to show a firm's financial position at a particular date. As such, Balance Sheets are used not only by the firm's own managers, but by outsiders as well. Those people supplying materials to the firm on credit will wish to know whether the business is in a position to pay its debts. Should the proprietor wish to borrow money from the bank, the bank will want to see just what financial state the business is in, and the Balance Sheet will provide a good guide.

A Balance Sheet is made up of two lists. The first is a list of what the business possesses. The second is a list of the firm's debts. Things owned by the business are called **assets** e.g. premises, machinery, cash at the bank. The monies owed by the business are referred to as the firm's **liabilities** e.g. money owed to suppliers. A Balance Sheet thus lists the firm's assets and its liabilities. The total of a firm's assets will always equal the total of its liabilities. This is the Balance Sheet equation.

It does not really matter how these lists are presented; they can be shown side by side, or one under the other. Balance Sheets A and B are presented in what is called the horizontal manner, whilst Balance Sheet C shows a vertical presentation. (See opposite)

In the United Kingdom presentation A tends to be used for the horizontal method, whereas in the United States of America presentation B is used, but it really does not matter and no particular method of presentation can be called the 'right' method. They are all equally acceptable.

```
+-----------------------------------------------------+
|                  Balance Sheet A                    |
|   +---------------+          +---------------+       |
|   |               |          |               |       |
|   |  Liabilities  |          |    Assets     |       |
|   |               |          |               |       |
|   +---------------+          +---------------+       |
|                                                      |
|                  Balance Sheet B                    |
|   +---------------+          +---------------+       |
|   |               |          |               |       |
|   |    Assets     |          |  Liabilities  |       |
|   |               |          |               |       |
|   +---------------+          +---------------+       |
|                                                      |
|                  Balance Sheet C                    |
|           +---------------------+                    |
|           |                     |                    |
|           |       Assets        |                    |
|           |                     |                    |
|           +---------------------+                    |
|           +---------------------+                    |
|           |                     |                    |
|           |     Liabilities     |                    |
|           |                     |                    |
|           +---------------------+                    |
+-----------------------------------------------------+
```

To see just how the Balance Sheet is constructed, the following example will be used. It describes Brown's activities when he founded the Numac Trading Co back in 195–.

January 1   C Brown began business with £20 000 in a business
bank account
2   Purchased premises for £12 000 paying by cheque
3   Purchased by cheque stock of goods for resale £2000
4   Sold half of the stock for £1500 cash

On 1 January, Brown began his business by opening a business
bank account with £20 000. This represents his investment in his
own business; in other words it is his capital. Capital is nearly
always a liability, since it is money owed by the business to the
proprietor. The corresponding asset on Brown's first Balance Sheet
will be £20 000 in the firm's bank account. The Balance Sheet will
therefore appear as below, with the total assets equal to the total
liabilities. Note that the opening of a *business* bank account signifies
that the accounts are concerned with the affairs of the business.
Brown may have had other bank accounts, but the records of
Numac Trading Co are concerned only with the firm's bank
account.

Balance Sheet as at 1 January 195-			
	£		£
Liabilities		*Assets*	
Capital	20 000	Bank	20 000

On the next day, Brown used some of this money to purchase
business premises. The figure for 'Bank' diminishes by £12 000 to
show the payment being made, while a new asset, 'Premises', of
£12 000 is introduced. The figure for capital remains unchanged;
nothing has happened either to increase or diminish Brown's
investment.

Balance Sheet as at 2 January 195-			
	£		£
Liabilities		*Assets*	
Capital	20 000	Premises	12 000
		Bank	8 000
	20 000		20 000

However, the assets which the business possesses have changed. Brown's investment is represented by £12 000 of premises and £8000 of money in the bank. If a friend asked him for a loan of £9000 he would not be able to oblige by using his business funds, for although he has £20 000 invested in the business, the business has only £8000 in the bank.

On 3 January, Brown buys items for re-sale and pays £2000 for them. Once more the list of assets changes. The item 'Bank' diminishes by £2000 and a third asset, 'Stock', is introduced. Note that the capital remains unchanged; nothing has happened to change it.

```
              Balance Sheet as at 3 January 195-

                      £                                    £
Liabilities                   Assets
Capital            20 000     Premises              12 000
                              Stock                  2 000
                              Bank                   6 000

                   _____                           _____
                   20 000                           20 000
                   ══════                           ══════
```

On 4 January, half of the stock was sold for cash, £1500 being received. The stock figure is reduced by £1000 − half of £2000 − to show the diminution of stock. A fourth asset, 'Cash', is introduced to show the £1500 flowing into the business.

```
              Balance Sheet as at 4 January 195-

                      £                                    £
Liabilities                   Assets
Capital            20 000     Premises              12 000
Profit                500     Stock                  1 000
                              Bank                   6 000
                              Cash                   1 500

                   _____                           _____
                   20 500                           20 500
                   ══════                           ══════
```

However, if the Balance Sheet is left like this, the total of the assets will be £500 more than the total of the liabilities. Clearly, something has gone wrong or has been omitted, since the total assets *always* equal the total liabilities.

The problem resolves itself as soon as we realise that the difference of £500 represents the profit earned on the items sold. Remember the stock figure was reduced by £1000 to show half of the stock leaving the business, but the asset 'Bank' was increased by £1500. Clearly, if items costing £1000 were sold for £1500 the firm has made a profit of £500, and who does this profit belong to? It belongs to the proprietor. His reason for setting up the business was to earn profits, and this £500 simply increases the debt which the business owes to the proprietor. The profit is added to the capital.

Anything which changes the *mixture* of assets or the *mixture* of liabilities will bring about changes on the Balance Sheet. So, too, will changes in the *value* of assets or the *value* of liabilities.

Firms do not simply buy and sell for cash; they often transact business on credit. In other words, goods or services change hands in response to a promise to pay at some future date. Let us now see how these are handled in our Balance Sheet example.

January 8 Bought goods on credit from Country Supplies £1200
       9 Sold goods on credit to G Mane £40. The goods had cost £20
     10 Paid Country Supplies by cheque the amount owing
     11 G Mane paid his amount by cheque

On 8 January Brown's business incurs a debt of £1200 − the money owing to Country Supplies. The business also acquires increased stock of £1200. Thus, on the Balance Sheet, the total liabilities increases and so, too, does the total of assets. The two lists

Balance Sheet as at 8 January 195-

	£		£
Capital	20 500	Premises	12 000
Creditor	1 200	Stock	2 200
(Country		Bank	6 000
Supplies)		Cash	1 500
	21 700		21 700

agree. The firm is now shown with two debts − one to the proprietor in terms of his capital, and one to the firm's **creditor**, Country Supplies. A **creditor** is one to whom the business owes money. The proprietor is, in this sense, a very special creditor.

On 9 January the firm sold goods to G Mane on credit for £40. To record this transaction, a number of Balance Sheet alterations are necessary. Firstly, since the items originally cost £20, the item 'Stock' must be reduced by this amount to reflect the fact that the goods have left the business. In return a new asset, 'Debtor', is created, for £40. Once again, the profit element must be allowed for by adding the profit of £20 on to the capital.

```
        Balance Sheet as at 9 January 195-
                       £                                £
Capital          20 500        Premises           12 000
Profit               20        Stock               2 180
                 -------       Debtor                 40
                 20 520        Bank                6 000
Creditor          1 200        Cash                1 500

                 -------                           -------
                 21 720                            21 720
                 =======                           =======
```

On 10 January the business settles its debt with Country Supplies. The Balance Sheet, therefore, shows the Bank figure reduced by £1200 and the Creditor figure reduced by a similar amount. The Creditor, thus, disappears from the Balance Sheet, and the Bank figure reduces to £4800.

```
        Balance Sheet as at 10 January 195-
                       £                                £
Capital          20 500        Premises           12 000
Profit               20        Stock               2 180
                 -------       Debtor                 40
                 20 520        Bank                4 800
                               Cash                1 500

                 -------                           -------
                 20 520                            20 520
                 =======                           =======
```

On 11 January Mane pays his account by cheque. He, therefore, ceases to be a debtor, and so he is removed from the Balance Sheet, while the Bank figure increases by the amount of his payment, £40.

```
              Balance Sheet as at 11 January 195-
                          £                                    £
Capital              20 520         Premises              12 000
                                    Stock                  2 180
                                    Bank                   4 840
                                    Cash                   1 500

                     _____                               _____
                     20 520                               20 520
                     ======                               ======
```

Why do debtors appear as assets in the Balance Sheet? Remember, assets are the things which a business possesses. In the case of a debtor, the business possesses a promise to pay. If the firm did not think that the customer would pay, then it would be silly to let him have goods. It is because the firm values the customer's promise, that it can enter this promise in the Balance Sheet as something worth owning.

Fixed and current items

Assets and liabilities are further classified as fixed and current items. Fixed assets are those assets which the firm has purchased with the intention of using within the business to generate profits; they have not been bought with the main intention of being resold. Fixed assets include items such as land and buildings, machinery, furniture and fittings, and vehicles.

Current assets are those possessions which the firm intends to turn into cash as soon as it can. The common current assets are stock, debtors, cash at the bank and cash in hand.

Note that assets are always listed in their *order of permanence*. Thus, the most permanent asset – land and buildings – will always appear first in the list of assets, while the least permanent — cash in hand — will appear at the bottom of the list. The order in which current assets appear in the Balance Sheet should always be stock, debtors, cash at bank and cash in hand.

The Balance Sheet does not specifically identify fixed liabilities, although capital itself is a fixed liability, since the business exists only so long as the proprietor has money invested in it. If he withdraws all his money the business will very likely cease, and since the proprietor's investment is money owed by the firm to him, capital remains essentially a fixed liability.

Current liabilities are those debts of the firm which are due for payment in the near future. They are essentially short-term debts. The most common current liability is trade creditors.

Numac Trading Co's Balance Sheet as at 9 January 195– can thus be rewritten to group separately, fixed and current assets and current liabilities. This is shown below.

NUMAC TRADING CO
Balance Sheet as at 9 January 195–

	£			£
Capital	20 500	*Fixed assets*		
Profit	20	Premises		12 000
	_____			
	20 520			
Current liabilities		*Current assets*		
Creditor	1 200	Stock	2 180	
		Debtors	40	
		Cash at bank	6 000	
		Cash in hand	1 500	
			_____	9 720
	_____			_____
	21 720			21 720

Note that the Balance Sheet shows a sub-total for current assets. Sub-totals should be shown for each of the four major sections of the Balance Sheet wherever these sections contain more than one figure.

Generally, the Balance Sheet equation can be written:

Capital + Current Liabilities = Fixed Assets + Current Assets

If we take the Balance Sheet for 11 January, it is quite feasible to write out the Balance Sheet as an equation:

	Capital	= Premises	+ Stock	+ Bank	+ Cash
	20 520	= 12 000	+ 2 180	+ 4 840	+ 1 500
	20 520	= 20 520			
or	Capital	− Bank	− Cash	= Premises	+ Stock
	20 520	− 4 840	− 1 500	= 12 000	+ 2 180
			14 180	= 14 180	

Remember: if you move an item from one side of the equation to the other, you change the sign.

If all the items are given except stock, the value of stock could be calculated:

Capital	− Premises	− Bank	− Cash	= Stock
20 520	− 12 000	− 4 840	− 1 500	= Stock
			2 180	= Stock

The value of the stock is £2 180

Similarly, if informed that Capital stood at £35 000, Stock at £4300, Bank at £1170 and Cash at £3330, the value of Premises can be determined:

Capital	− Bank	− Cash	− Stock	= Premises
35 000	− 1 170	− 3 330	− 4 300	= Premises
			26 200	= Premises

The value of the premises is £26 200

Summary

On completion of this unit plus practice at the exercises you should be able to:

1 Define the nature and purpose of a Balance Sheet. (E1)
2 Produce simple Balance Sheets from information supplied. (E1)

Exercises

1 In your own words explain the meaning of:

assets   debtor
liabilities   creditor
current assets   capital
current liabilities   order of permanence
fixed assets

2 Complete the gaps in the following table:

	Capital	Current liabilities	Fixed assets	Current assets
	£	£	£	£
a.	?	5 000	14 000	11 000
b.	15 000	3 200	?	6 500
c.	28 300	?	20 700	15 200
d.	46 700	12 800	29 400	?
e.	32 160	9 720	?	23 330

3 Copy out the following list, and enter against each item whether it is an asset, A, or a liability, L:

fixtures and fittings   loan from the bank
stock of materials   premises
debt owed to a supplier   profit
money in the bank

4 From the following information, draw up the Balance Sheet of D Jones, a trader, at the end of each day's activity.

Jan 1 Began business with £20 000 in a business bank account
     2 Paid cheque £15 000 to purchase premises
     3 Bought equipment by cheque £3000
     4 Bought stock of goods valued at £6000 for resale; £1000 was paid for by cheque, the remainder was bought on credit
     5 Sold half of the stock for £5000 cash

5 Use the following information to produce daily Balance Sheets for A Green, a trader:

Feb 17 Opened a business bank account with £40 000
     18 Paid by cheque for premises £18 000 and equipment £5000
     19 Bought stock valued at £7000; £5000 was paid for by cheque, the remainder was bought on credit

20 Sold half the stock for £3000 cash
21 Paid creditors by cheque
22 Sold stock valued at £500 for £600, the goods being sold on credit

6 The following daily Balance Sheets refer to the business of D Dock, a grocer. You are required to explain carefully what has happened on each day.

```
        Balance Sheet as at November 1 19-1
                      £                              £
Capital           30 000       Premises          12 000
                               Fixtures           2 000
                               Bank              16 000

                  ───────                        ───────
                  30 000                          30 000
                  ═══════                         ═══════


        Balance Sheet as at November 2 19-1
                      £                              £
Capital           30 000       Premises          12 000
Creditors          2 000       Fixtures           2 000
                               Stock              5 000
                               Bank              13 000

                  ───────                        ───────
                  32 000                          32 000
                  ═══════                         ═══════


        Balance Sheet as at November 3 19-1
                      £                              £
Capital           30 000       Premises          12 000
Profit             1 500       Fixtures           2 000
                  ───────      Stock              2 500
                  31 500       Debtors            4 000
Creditors          1 000       Bank              12 000

                  ───────                        ───────
                  32 500                          32 500
                  ═══════                         ═══════
```

7 Rewrite the following Balance Sheet, correcting any errors you may find.

Balance Sheet of W Baker for the year ended 31 December 19-2				
	£			£
Creditors 7 000		Stock		5 000
Less		Premises		30 000
Debtors 2 000		Machinery		18 000
	5 000	Bank		3 000
Profit	2 000			56 000
		Less Capital		50 000
				6 000
		Cash		1 000
	7 000			7 000

8 Why are debtors listed as assets?

9 Why does capital appear in the list of liabilities?

10 What is the purpose of a Balance Sheet, and how does it do this?

11 Why should a Balance Sheet be headed 'as at' a certain date?

12 What is meant by the Balance Sheet equation?

3 Cash transactions

Although a form of accounting system can be developed using Balance Sheets, it is clear that in practice such a system would be difficult to operate. One can well imagine how a large firm such as Marks and Spencer or British Leyland might find difficulties if their accounting system was comprised solely of Balance Sheets. Clearly, some extension is needed of the simplified system developed in Unit 1.

Double entry accounting derives its name from the fact that each business transaction appears twice in the accounting record. It does so, not simply to duplicate matters, but to reflect the dual effect that each transaction has on the firm.

If you buy a record from a shop, two things happen. Firstly, the shop's stock of records diminishes, and secondly, its stock of cash increases. You leave the cash in the shop, and take the record away.

To help in recording this dual effect, the accounts are kept on specially ruled sheets of ledger paper, or folios. The paper is divided into two sides. The left-hand side is referred to as the debit side, while the right-hand side is known as the credit side.

The word debit merely indicates left and credit indicates right. Sometimes these terms are abbreviated to Dr indicating debit and Cr indicating credit.

The general rule is that each transaction is entered on the debit side of one account, and on the credit side of another. One only needs to know:

1 Which two accounts to use?
2 Which side of each of the accounts to use?

Whenever you are asked to compile a set of accounts from raw information, you should always ask yourself the above questions for each transaction.

Capital

Consider the case of C Brown. He began his business on 1 January 195– with £20 000 in his business bank account. It is therefore necessary to record in the ledger the asset, Cash at bank and the liability, Capital.

Entries recording the *increase* of an *asset* appear on the *debit* side of the asset account, while entries recording an *increase* of a *liability* appear on the *credit* side of the liability account.

The two accounts needed to record the setting up of the business will be the Capital Account and the Bank Account. A debit entry is made on the Bank Account to show the asset increasing, while a credit entry is made on the Capital Account to show the liability increasing. The basic rule of double entry accounting has been obeyed: the ledger shows a debit entry and a corresponding credit entry.

Capital			
			£
	Jan	1 Bank	20 000

Bank			
		£	
Jan	1 Capital	20 000	

Note, too, that against each figure is written the account wherein the second entry can be found. Thus, 'Bank' is written in the Capital Account because the corresponding entry can be found in the Bank Account. Similarly, 'Capital' is written in the Bank Account.

Fixed assets

On 2 January Brown bought business premises, paying £12 000 by cheque. The purchase and sale of fixed assets do not appear in either a Purchases or a Sales Account. These two accounts record only the purchase and sale of goods bought specifically for resale. Fixed assets are bought for use within the business, and while they may be sold at some future date, they are not bought solely for that purpose.

In Brown's case, the premises were purchased with the intention of using them within the business. Hence they are classed as fixed assets. The two accounts necessary to record this transaction are

1 Bank Account, and
2 Premises Account

Bank				
		£		£
Jan 1 Capital	20 000		Jan 2 Premises	12 000

Premises		
		£
Jan 2 Bank	12 000	

When Brown writes out his cheque, it is an instruction to his bank to pay some of his money out of his bank account. It is, therefore, necessary for the Bank Account to show this money leaving the business. When Brown introduced £20 000 into the business, an entry was made on the debit side of the Bank Account. Since he is now paying £12 000 out of the business, the Bank Account must be credited with £12 000.

While the asset Cash at bank has been reduced, the asset Premises has been increased. As was seen above, an increase in an asset is recorded by making a debit entry on that asset's account. The Premises Account is, therefore, debited with £12 000, and the double entry is complete.

Purchases

Items bought for resale *are* recorded in a Purchases Account. Thus, when Brown bought items on 3 January for resale, paying £2000 by cheque, the transaction is recorded in the:

1   Bank Account, and
2   Purchases Account

```
                                Bank
                     £                                        £
Jan  1 Capital    20 000        Jan  2 Premises  12 000
                                Jan  3 Purchases  2 000
```

```
                              Purchases
                     £
Jan  3 Bank        2 000
```

Again, Brown is spending money from his bank account, so once more the Bank Account is credited with £2000. The corresponding debit entry appears on the Purchases Account.

Generally speaking, entries on the Purchases Account will nearly always appear on the debit side.

Sales

When, on 4 January, Brown sells items for £1500 cash, the entries are made in:

1   Sales Account, and
2   Cash Account

The ledger accounts distinguish very carefully between goods purchased for resale — which appear in the Purchases Account — and goods actually sold — which appear in the Sales Account. The two accounts are separate accounts, and they remain so.

Since purchases are recorded on the debit side of the Purchases Account, and since sales are the opposite of purchases, it is not surprising to find that sales appear on the credit side of the Sales Account.

The entry for 4 January thus appears as a credit entry on the Sales Account, with the corresponding debit entry on the Cash Account. Note that so far as the Bank and Cash Accounts are concerned, money coming in is entered on the debit side, while money going out is entered on the credit side. This is always so.

Sales			
			£
	Jan 4 Cash		1 500

Cash			
	£		
Jan 4 Sales	1 500		

Generally speaking, entries on the Sales Account will nearly always appear on the credit side.

Expenses

There are a number of items which do not appear in Balance Sheets, but which nevertheless have to be recorded in the firm's ledgers. Two of these items are Expenses and Income. They do not appear as Balance Sheet items, so the example used in Unit 2 cannot be employed as an illustration. It is necessary to introduce other examples.

Suppose that during the first week of his business, Brown paid the following expenses:

Jan 4   Rates by cheque £250
5   Insurance by cheque £120
6   Wages by cash £40

Each expense will be entered on the debit side of a separate expense account. Separate accounts are necessary so that the firm's managers can see just how much is being spent on particular expenses.

In this example, the accounts would appear as on page 35, with the expense accounts being debited, and the Bank and Cash Accounts credited, to show the money leaving the firm.

```
                            Rates
          ──────────────────────────────────────────
                            £
  Jan   4 Bank             250
```

```
                          Insurance
          ──────────────────────────────────────────
                            £
  Jan   5 Bank             120
```

```
                            Wages
          ──────────────────────────────────────────
                            £
  Jan   6 Cash              40
```

```
                            Bank
          ──────────────────────────────────────────
                     £                              £
  Jan  1 Capital  20 000      Jan   2 Premises  12 000
                                    3 Purchases  2 000
                                    4 Rates        250
                                    5 Insurance    120
```

```
                            Cash
          ──────────────────────────────────────────
                     £                              £
  Jan  4 Sales    1 500      Jan   6 Wages          40
```

When an expense is increased, the entry appears on the debit side of that expense account, so that any expense incurred will *always* appear on the debit side of the relevant expense account.

Income

Revenue from selling goods might not be the only form of income which the business has. The proprietor may let the flat above his shop, he may invest some of the firm's profits in the shares of a public company, or he may simply put surplus cash into a bank deposit account.

In each case, the business will receive some form of income: rent received, dividends received or interest received. The proprietor will enter each form of income in a separate account, and income earned will *always* appear on the credit side of the relevant income account.

If Brown earned extra income as below, the accounts would appear as follows;

Jan 8   Received rent from tenant of flat £50 cash
   9   Received dividends by cheque £200

Rent Received		
		£
	Jan 8 Cash	50

Dividends Received		
		£
	Jan 9 Bank	200

Cash				
	£			£
Jan 4 Sales	1 500	Jan 6 Wages		40
8 Rent received	50			

```
                           Bank
                 £                                    £
Jan  1 Capital   20 000     Jan  2 Premises  12 000
     9 Dividends                 3 Purchases  2 000
       received      200          4 Rates        250
                                  5 Insurance    120
```

Drawings

A proprietor sets up a business in order to earn profits, and periodically he will calculate what profit has been made. However, the proprietor will have to pay his own personal expenses regularly: *his* tradesmen will not wait to be paid until he has calculated his profit.

Most proprietors, therefore, will withdraw money from the business during the year in lieu of profits so that they themselves can live. Such withdrawals are called **drawings** and they are recorded in a separate Drawings Account.

Assume that on 10 January Brown withdrew from the business bank account £100 for his own private use. This withdrawal reduces the debt which the firm owes to him. The entry on the Drawings Account will, therefore, appear on the debit side, with the corresponding entry on the credit side of the Bank Account.

```
                           Bank
                 £                                    £
Jan  1 Capital   20 000     Jan  2 Premises  12 000
     9 Dividends                  3 Purchases  2 000
       received      200          4 Rates        250
                                  5 Insurance    120
                                 10 Drawings     100
```

```
                         Drawings
                 £
Jan 10 Bank      100
```

Had Brown withdrawn £100 in cash for his own use, then the Drawings Account would still have been debited with £100, but the corresponding credit entry would have appeared on the Cash Account.

If Brown had taken £100 of goods from stock for his own use, the Drawings Account would have been debited, and the Purchases Account credited. This is one of the very few occasions when credit entries appear on the Purchases Account.

Drawings		
	£	
Jan 10 Purchases	100	

Purchases				
	£			£
Jan 3 Bank	2 000	Jan 10 Drawings		100

A worked example

It is now possible to bring together in one example all the separate items that have been discussed above. Follow the example through carefully, noting the entries necessary to record:

a capital and drawings
b purchase of assets − by cheque and/or cash
c purchase of goods − by cheque and/or cash
d sale of goods − by cheque and/or cash
e expenses
f income

Aug 1 K Osborne began business by depositing £24 000 in a business bank account
   2 Bought furniture £3200 and delivery van £4600, in both cases paying by cheque
   3 Bought goods for resale £7300 by cheque; sold items for cash £178

4 Bought further goods for resale, cash £52; paid cash £46 for display cabinet

5 Paid wages, cash £56; sales by cheque £89; drawings by cheque £100

6 Paid rent by cheque £200; cash sales £140; received rent from tenant £20 cash; bought goods for resale £1700 by cheque; took goods for personal use £30

Capital

			£
		Aug 1 Bank	24 000

Bank

	£			£
Aug 1 Capital	24 000	Aug 2 Furniture		3 200
5 Sales	89	Delivery van		4 600
		3 Purchases		7 300
		5 Drawings		100
		6 Rent		200
		Purchases		1 700

Cash

	£		£
Aug 3 Sales	178	Aug 4 Purchases	52
6 Sales	140	Furniture	46
Rent received	20	5 Wages	56

Furniture

	£
Aug 2 Bank	3 200
4 Cash	46

Delivery Van

	£
Aug 2 Bank	4 600

Purchases

			£				£
Aug	3	Bank	7 300	Aug	6	Drawings	30
	4	Cash	52				
	6	Bank	1 700				

Sales

					£
			Aug	3 Cash	178
				5 Bank	89
				6 Cash	140

Wages

			£
Aug	5	Cash	56

Drawings

			£
Aug	5	Bank	100
	6	Purchases	30

Rent

			£
Aug	6	Bank	200

Rent Received

			£
		Aug	6 Cash	20

Summary

On completion of this unit plus practice at the exercises you should be able to:

1 Classify and record assets, liabilities, income and expenses in the ledger.
2 Record withdrawals of money and goods by the proprietor for his own use.

Exercises

1 Explain in your own words the meaning of:
ledger   debit
folio   credit
account   double entry
drawings

Questions 2, 3 and 4: state which account you would debit, and which you would credit to record the following transactions:

		Account	
		Dr	Cr
2 *a*	Began business with £40 000 in the bank		
b	Paid by cheque for goods £5000		
c	Sold goods for cash £100		
d	Sold goods, received cheque £200		
e	Purchased further items for resale £800 cheque		
f	Took goods for owner's use £70		
3 *a*	Began business with £30 000 in the bank		
b	Bought fixtures by cheque £8000		
c	Paid wages by cheque £200		
d	Bought goods for resale £1200 cheque		
e	Sold goods for cash £300		
f	Transferred £200 from bank account to Cash Account		
g	Paid cleaners £40 cash		
h	Received rent from tenant of flat £36		
i	Withdrew £22 cash for owner's use		

4 *a*   Opened a business bank account with £50 000

   b   Purchased premises by cheque £20 000

   c   Bought stock £3600 by cheque

   d   Sold goods for cash £130

   e   Sold goods, received cheques £420

   f   Purchased stocks for cash £100

   g   Withdrew £150 by cheque for personal use

5   Why are transactions entered twice in a firm's accounts?

Questions 6, 7 and 8: enter the transactions in the appropriate ledger accounts.

6   April   1   Began business with £9000 in the bank

            2   Purchased by cheque stocks for resale £2000

            5   Bought fixtures by cheque £150

            7   Sold goods for cash £40

            9   Cash sales £75

          10   Paid rent by cheque £50

          11   Cash sales £54

          16   Paid cash for stock £100

          20   Cheques banked for goods sold £230

          24   Paid £15 cash for cleaning materials

          28   Cash sales £93

          29   Goods withdrawn for owner's use £30

7   July   16   Began business with £10 000 cash

          17   Transferred £8000 from cash to business bank account

          18   Purchased equipment for use in the business £1650 by cheque

          21   Paid by cheque for stocks £570

          22   Paid cash for delivery van £1500; paid wages, cash £50

          24   Cash sales £67

          27   Paid the following expenses by cheque: rent £120, insurance £217

          28   Cash sales £114; paid £7 cash for postage stamps

          30   Cash sales £98; paid wages £50 cash; drawings by cheque £20

8 March 1 Started business with £24 000 in the bank
          2 Paid by cheque for premises £14 000, furniture and fittings £670
          3 Purchased stocks by cheque £760
          4 Cash sales £105
          5 Cash sales £192; paid for petrol by cash £10
          6 Paid wages by cash £40; received rent from tenant of flat, cash £30
          8 Sales paid for by cheques £84; cash drawings £15
          9 Purchased stocks by cash £50
         10 Cash sales £132; paid for petrol £12 cash
         11 Paid window cleaner, cash £2; paid for stationery by cheque £22.
         13 Wages paid by cash £40; received rent, cheque £30

9 Examine the following account, and explain carefully the significance of each entry:

Bank					
		£			£
Nov 1 Capital	17	000	Nov 2 Premises	11	000
8 Sales		240	Fixtures	1	400
17 Sales		260	5 Purchases	2	700
Rent		80	8 Wages		120
			14 Cash		300
			Drawings		520

10 Explain the meaning of each entry in the following account:

Cash					
		£			£
Sept 1 Capital	8	000	Sept 2 Bank	6	000
5 Sales		78	4 Purchases	1	000
7 Sales		112	8 Wages		65
Rent		20	9 Drawings		93
			Rent		80

4 Balancing the accounts— the Trial Balance

From time to time the managers of a business will need to know what the total sales figure is for a given period. They will need this figure to compare actual sales with planned sales and so assess performance: does the firm need to employ a more aggressive sales strategy or are matters progressing satisfactorily?

In order to derive a total sales figure, the Sales Account will need to be totalled. It would, of course, be tedious and would increase the risk of error if this were done only at infrequent intervals, and since the managers of the firm are likely to demand regularly updated information, it is common in business for the accounts to be totalled at least monthly and often weekly. An accounting period represents the time covered by the information; thus, an accounting period can be a week, a month, three months, six months or a year. This totalling of the accounts is referred to as 'balancing the accounts'. Reproduced below is the Sales Account from Unit 3.

Sales			
			£
Aug	4	Cash	178
	5	Cash	89
	6	Cash	140

The total sales figure for the week is £407 (see above). In order to balance the account according to accounting conventions the figures on the credit side are added, and the total written underneath, as follows.

```
                          Sales
                                                           £
                        Aug   4  Cash                     178
                              5  Cash                      89
                              6  Cash                     140
                                                          ———
                                                          407
                                                          ═══
```

Next, the two sides of the account are made to 'balance' i.e. they are made to add up to the same figure. In order to make both sides of the Sales Account equal, £407 must be added to the debit side, as below. Finally, in order that it abides by the fundamental rule of double

```
                             Sales
                      £                                    £
   Aug  6  Balance    407    Aug   4  Cash                178
                                   5  Cash                 89
                                   6  Cash                140
                     ———                                  ———
                     407                                  407
                     ═══                                  ═══
```

entry accounting, for each debit entry there must be a corresponding credit entry. This is achieved by transferring the balance of £407 to the credit side of the Sales Account, beneath the current week's total, as below. The account is now ready to begin another week.

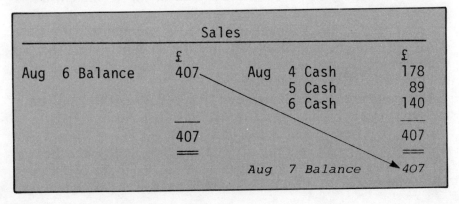

```
                             Sales
                      £                                    £
   Aug  6  Balance    407    Aug   4  Cash                178
                                   5  Cash                 89
                                   6  Cash                140
                     ———                                  ———
                     407                                  407
                     ═══                                  ═══
                             Aug   7  Balance             407
```

The purpose of the double lines under the totals is to signify that they *are* totals. Just like double white lines in the middle of the road, these lines should never be crossed. When next any calculations are performed on the Sales Account, omit all figures above these lines.

Note that the assumption is made that the balance on the debit side closes one week — August 6 — whilst the second balance opens the next week — August 7.

The total figures for Purchases and for the various expenses will also be required. If the Purchases Account has to be balanced the sequence is similar. Again, the Purchases Account from Unit 3 will be used.

			Purchases				
			£				£
Aug	3	Bank	7 300	Aug	6	Drawings	30
	4	Cash	52			Balance	9 022
	6	Bank	1 700				
			9 052				9 052
Aug	7	Balance	9 022				

The figures appear on the debit side this time, so in order to make the two sides agree, £9022 has to be added to the credit side. The double entry for this is the debit entry of £9022 dated August 7.

When the second balance is brought down onto the credit side of the account, as in the Sales Account, the account is said to have a **credit balance**. In other words, the total of the credit entries is greater than the total of the debit entries.

Conversely, when the second balance is brought down on the debit side, as in the Purchases Account, the account is said to have a **debit balance**. In such cases, the total of the debit entries is greater than the total of the credit entries.

This same principle applies when an account has entries on both the debit and the credit sides. Consider the Cash Account in Unit 3.

During the week, £338 was paid in: £178 + £140 + £20 = £338, whilst £154 (£52 + £46 + £56) was paid out. In order to make the two sides of this account balance, £184 must be added to the credit side. The double entry for this £184 is the balance which is brought down to the debit side to open the following period. This £184 is, in fact, the amount of cash still held by the firm: it is the difference between what was paid in – £338 – and what was paid out – £154.

£338 – £154 = £184

```
                              Cash
                         £                              £
Aug  4 Sales            178    Aug  4 Purchases        52
     6 Sales            140         Furniture          46
       Rent                       5 Wages              56
       received          20       6 Balance           184
                        ───                           ───
                        338                            338
                        ═══                            ═══
Aug  7 Balance          184
```

It is now possible to balance all of the accounts used in Unit 3. They would appear as on pages 48–50. It is not usually necessary to balance one line accounts. Thus, in the example, the Capital and Rent Accounts are not balanced. If, for some reason, it was felt necessary to balance a one line account, it would appear as:

```
                             Capital
                        £                              £
Aug  6 Balance       24000    Aug  1 Bank          24 000
                     ═════                          ══════
                              Aug  7 Balance        24000
```

On the Bank Account, the credit side totals £17 100, whilst there is an entry on the debit side of £24 089. Thus, in order to make the two sides equal, it is necessary to add only £6989 to the credit side. The balance brought down to the debit side thus shows that the firm still has £6989 in the bank. At the beginning of the week, £24 000 was paid into the bank. During the week a further £89 was received by way of sales, whereas £17 100 was spent, leaving £6989 still in the account:

£24 089 – £17 100 = £6989

48

In general, the following accounts have debit balances:
  A ssets
  L osses
  E xpenses
The following accounts have credit balances:
  L iabilities
  I ncome
  P rofit

	Capital		
			£
	Aug	1 Bank	24 000

		Bank			
		£			£
Aug	1 Capital	24 000	Aug	2 Furniture	3 200
	5 Sales	89		Van	4 600
				3 Purchases	7 300
				5 Drawings	100
				6 Rent	200
				Purchases	1 700
				Balance	*6 989*
		24 089			24 089
Aug	*7 Balance*	*6 989*			

		Cash·			
		£			£
Aug	4 Sales	178	Aug	4 Purchases	52
	6 Sales	140		Furniture	46
	Rent			5 Wages	56
	received	20		*6 Balance*	*184*
		338			338
Aug	*7 Balance*	*184*			

Furniture

			£				£
Aug	2	Bank	3 200	Aug	6	*Balance*	*3 246*
	4	Cash	46				
			3 246				3 246
Aug	*7*	*Balance*	*3 246*				

Van

			£
Aug	2	Bank	4 600

Purchases

			£				£
Aug	3	Bank	7 300	Aug	6	Drawings	30
	4	Cash	52			*Balance*	*9 022*
	6	Bank	1 700				
			9 052				9 052
Aug	*7*	*Balance*	*9 022*				

Sales

			£				£
Aug	*6*	*Balance*	*407*	Aug	4	Cash	178
					5	Bank	89
					6	Cash	140
			407				407
				Aug	*7*	*Balance*	*407*

Wages

			£
Aug	5	Cash	56

Drawings

		£			£
Aug	5 Bank	100	Aug 6 Balance		130
	6 Purchases	30			
		130			130
Aug	7 Balance	130			

Rent

		£
Aug	6 Bank	200

Rent Received

		£
	Aug 6 Cash	20

The Trial Balance

These balances are not only useful for informing the accountant of the total of particular items at various times; they can also be used as a form of check upon the accounting records themselves.

Remember, each transaction is entered twice in the accounts: once on the debit side and once on the credit side. If the task of entering the figures has been done properly, the total of the debit entries should equal the total of the credit entries.

Shown at the top of page 51 is a list of the debit and credit *entries* for the example used in Unit 3.

Notice that the total of the debit entries, £41 711, is the same as the total for the credit entries.

```
Trial Balance as at 6th August 19-1
                          £            £
Capital                             24 000
Bank                  24 089        17 100
Cash                     338           154
Furniture              3 246
Van                    4 600
Purchases              9 052            30
Sales                                  407
Drawings                 130
Wages                     56
Rent paid                200
Rent received                           20

                      41 711        41 711
                      ======        ======
```

The same effect is obtained if, instead of listing the *entries*, the *balances* are listed. Obviously, using this approach, the totals of the columns will be different from the totals derived above: £24 427 instead of £41 711, but at least the total of the debit columns still equals the total of the credit columns: they *both* add to £24 427 and this is all we seek to achieve — matching totals.

```
Trial Balance as at 6th August 19-1
                          £            £
Capital                             24 000
Bank                   6 989
Cash                     184
Furniture              3 246
Van                    4 600
Purchases              9 022
Sales                                  407
Drawings                 130
Wages                     56
Rent paid                200
Rent received                           20

                      24 427        24 427
                      ======        ======
```

This listing of the debit balances and the credit balances is known as the **Trial Balance.**

The Trial Balance is used to check the *arithmetical* accuracy of the accounts. The fact that it balances i.e. the total debits equal the total credits, does not mean that the accounts are correct. There are some mistakes which the Trial Balance will not reveal.

For instance, if a transaction is not entered on any account at all, there will be no record of it in the ledger. This **error of omission** will remain undetected by the Trial Balance.

Again, if the entries are completely reversed, the Trial Balance will still agree, and yet the accounts will not be correct. **Reversal of entries** means that an entry which should appear on the debit side has been made on the credit side and vice versa.

If an entry has been made on the correct side, but in the wrong *class* of account, the Trial Balance will not reveal the mistake. Thus, if an expense is debited to an asset account, since both assets and expenses are debit items, no mistake will be shown. This is known as an **error of principle**.

An entry might also be made in the correct *type* of account, but on the wrong *individual* account. For example, an expense might be debited to Heating instead of to Electricity. Both are expense accounts. This is an **error of commission**.

Transposition of figures is another frequent mistake which may be hidden by the Trial Balance. An entry may be made for £354 instead of for £345. If the wrong figure is entered on both debit and credit sides of the records, the Trial Balance will not reveal the error.

Finally, there are occasions when, by sheer coincidence, two independent mistakes cancel each other out. Such **compensating errors** will leave the Trial Balance still in balance.

The Trial Balance, whilst useful as a check upon the arithmetical accuracy of the accounts, still has severe limitations.

Summary

On completion of this unit plus practice at the exercises you should be able to:

1　Balance a set of simple accounts. (G2)
2　Produce from these simple accounts a Trial Balance. (G2)
3　Describe the function and limitations of a Trial Balance. (G2)

Exercises

To meet Objective G2.

1   Explain the meaning of the following accounting terms:
balancing an account   debit balance
credit balance   Trial Balance

2   Enter the following transactions in the appropriate ledger accounts.

Sept   1   Cash sales £90
       3   Cash purchases £40
       4   Cash sales £50
       5   Cash purchases £30
       6   Cash sales £120

Balance the accounts as at 6 September, and continue:

Sept   8   Sold goods, cheques banked £200
       9   Purchased goods by cheque £50
      11   Cash sales £60
      13   Purchased goods by cheque £90

Balance the accounts as at 13 September.

Questions 3, 4, 5 and 6: enter the transactions in the appropriate accounts, balance the accounts, and produce a Trial Balance.

3   Oct   1   Opened a business bank account with £10 000
          2   Bought equipment by cheque £1000
          3   Bought stock by cheque £500
          4   Sold goods for cash £70
          5   Banked cheques for goods sold £140
          6   Paid cash for purchases £50
          8   Paid the following expenses by cheque: rent £70, rates
              £290, insurance £180
          9   Paid for delivery van by cheque £2700; cash sales £132
         11   Cash sales £210; postage paid by cash £5
         13   Paid for purchases by cheque £270; paid for heating oil
              £148 by cheque

4 Dec 14 Opened business with £12 000 in the bank
        15 Paid by cheque for equipment £3500 and stocks £2600
        16 Cash sales £78
        17 Cash sales £92; paid telephone bill by cheque £85
        18 Purchased goods by cheque £400; paid cash for delivery charges £4
        19 Cash sales £130; rent paid by cash £56; wages paid cash £30
        23 Banked cheques for goods sold £474; cash sales £120
        25 Cash sales £132; paid cash for purchases £81
        26 Paid expenses in cash: wages £30, rent £56

5 Feb 9 Began business with £5000 cash
        10 Paid cash for equipment £700, and transferred remainder of cash to bank account
        12 Purchased stock by cheque £400
        13 Cash sales £150; paid for petrol, cash £12
        14 Cash sales £230; purchased stock by cheque £300
        16 Transferred £200 from cash to bank account
        17 Paid heating and lighting bills by cheque £70; cash sales £194
        18 Bought office furniture by cheque £1200
        20 Cash sales £246; paid by cash for: rent £130, petrol £14, postage £8

6 Nov 2 Opened business bank account with £20 000
        3 Paid for business premises by cheque £12 000
        4 Paid for purchases by cheque £3000; cash sales £110
        5 Cash sales £191; paid for furniture and fittings by cheque £1790
        6 Cash sales £140; paid wages in cash £50; received rent from tenant £66 cash
        8 Cash sales £211; cash purchases £120
        9 Paid: rates by cheque £370, insurance by cheque £274
        11 Cash sales £182; paid cash for motor licence £60, and for advertising £21
        13 Cash sales £250; banked cheques for goods sold £310; paid wages by cheque £50; received cheque from tenant for rent £66

7 Rewrite the following in the form of a Trial Balance:

	£
Capital	10 000
Bank	2 000
Cash	60
Sales	660
Purchases	1 240
Motor van	1 100
Premises	6 000
Wages	260

8 The following Trial Balance is incorrectly drawn up. Rewrite it correcting any errors.

BEL JOY CO

Trial Balance
for month ended 31 December 19-1

	£	£
Wages		160
Fixtures	1 700	
Capital	21 300	
Insurance	200	
Cash	120	
Sales		8 660
Purchases		5 200
Premises		6 980
Insurance	300	
Balance		2 620
	23 620	23 620

9 What is the purpose of the Trial Balance, and how does it achieve this?

10 What mistakes will the Trial Balance not reveal, and why?

5 Credit transactions

Thus far, consideration has been given only to those situations where goods have been paid for at the time of purchase or sale. Much of business, however, is conducted on the basis of credit. In other words, items or services are bought and sold in exchange for a promise to pay in the future. This method of operation gives rise to **debtors** and to **creditors**.

Unit 2 showed that debtors are included as assets on the Balance Sheet, while creditors appear in the list of liabilities. Remember, an asset is something owned by a business, whilst a liability is something owed by the business.

In the case of a debtor, the thing owned is the customer's promise to pay. The business obviously regards this promise as being of value, and hence lists it as being a thing worth possessing. If the firm did not value the customer's promise to pay − if it thought that the debt would not be paid − it would be foolish to allow the goods or services to leave the business.

A similar principle applies to creditors. Here the firm has bought items against a promise to pay in the future. Such outstanding promises are debts of the firm, and as such they feature in the list of items owed by the firm.

Debtors

Assume the business makes the following sales on credit:

June 4   Sold goods on credit to C Hardy £150
June 6   Sold more goods to C Hardy on credit £90
June 7   Sold goods on credit to T Dickens £220

The accounts would appear as in Fig. 1a.

Since goods sold on credit by the firm create debtors, and since debtors are classed as assets, then the entries on the debtors'

Figure 1a Credit sales

Sales

	£
June 4 C Hardy	150
June 6 C Hardy	90
June 7 T Dickens	220

C Hardy

		£
June 4	Sales	150
6	Sales	90

T Dickens

		£
June 7	Sales	220

Figure 1b Cash sales

Sales

	£
June 4 Cash	150
June 6 Cash	90
June 7 Cash	220

Cash

		£
June 4	Sales	150
June 6	Sales	90
June 7	Sales	220

accounts appear on the debit side. Note, too, that separate accounts are kept for each debtor. This enables the firm to see the position of each individual customer: who has paid and who has not.

The entries on the Sales Account appear on the credit side, as normal. Compare these entries with those necessary to record cash sales (Fig. 1b). It will be seen that only when items are sold on credit is it necessary to have an account for each customer. When items are paid for, it is simply necessary to use a Cash or a Bank Account.

Note, too, that in accounting examples, if no mention is made of payment, then it is usual to assume that the transaction has been conducted on a credit basis. Where cash, cheques or any other form of payment is made at the time of sale, a separate account for the customer is not necessary. Thus, the instruction:

'Sold goods to C Hardy for cash £150'

would demand an entry on the debit side of the Cash Account. There is no need to make an entry on Hardy's Account, since the items have already been paid for.

In fact, if an entry was made on Hardy's Account, then he would eventually be sent a bill for goods for which he had already paid!

Creditors

When the purchase of goods is on credit, then it is necessary to open a separate account for each creditor. These accounts would then be credited with the amount of each purchase, whilst the Purchases Account would be debited.

Thus, the following transactions would appear as in Fig. 2a:

June 21   Bought items for resale from BJ Co £600
June 23   Bought further items of stock on credit from BJ Co £300
June 24   Purchased on credit goods for resale from Factum Ltd £400

If the items had been paid for by cheque, instead of being bought on credit, the entries would have appeared as in Fig. 2b. Note that in this case it would not be necessary to have separate accounts for each supplier. These are needed only when goods are bought on credit so that it can be seen just how much the firm owes to each individual supplier.

Figure 2a Credit purchases

BJ Co

		£
June 21	Purchases	600
23	Purchases	300

Factum Ltd

		£
June 24	Purchases	400

Purchases

			£
June 21	BJ Co		600
23	BJ Co		300
24	Factum Ltd	400

Figure 2b Cheque purchases

Bank

		£
June 21	Purchases	600
23	Purchases	300
24	Purchases	400

Purchases

		£
June 21	Bank	600
23	Bank	300
24	Bank	400

Payment

When a customer pays part of his debt to the firm, he reduces his indebtedness. The amount of the asset Debtors is diminished, while the asset Cash or Bank − depending on the method of payment − is increased.

Assume that on 30 June, Hardy pays all of his outstanding debt by cheque, whilst Dickens pays only £100 of his by cash. The accounts would appear as follows:

		C Hardy		
	£			£
June 4 Sales	150	June 30 Bank		240
6 Sales	90			
	240			240

		T Dickens		
	£			£
June 7 Sales	220	June 30 Cash		100
		Balance		120
	220			220
July 1 Balance	120			

Bank	
£	
June 30 C Hardy	240

Cash	
£	
June 30 T Dickens	100

Hardy's debt is removed by entering the amount which he has paid on the credit side of his account − the double entry appearing on the debit side of the Bank Account. Thus, at the end of the month, the debit and the credit sides of his account are equal, so there is no outstanding figure to carry forward into the following month of July.

However, Dickens pays only £100 from his total debt. This is credited to his account i.e. entered on the credit side of his account, with the double entry appearing on the debit side of the Cash Account. When his account is balanced at the end of June, £120 is carried down to the debit side. His account is said to have a 'debit balance', and this is where the term **debtor** comes from: debit − debtor meaning one who owes a debt.

Whenever a personal account i.e. one carrying the name of a person or a business, has a debit balance, it signifies that the person or firm is a debtor. In the case of Dickens, he is a debtor for £120 at the beginning of July.

Whenever a firm pays one of its suppliers, it reduces the amount it owes. Thus, the liability Creditors is reduced, and so too is the asset Cash or Bank, depending upon how the creditor is paid.

Suppose that on 30 June, Numac Trading Co pays £500 by cheque to BJ Co and £400 by cheque to Factum Ltd. The entries would appear as below:

```
                              BJ Co
                         £                                £
June 30 Bank            500     June 21 Purchases        600
             Balance    400          23 Purchases        300
                        ───                              ───
                        900                              900
                        ═══                              ═══
                                July  1 Balance          400

                            Factum Ltd
                         £                                £
June 30 Bank            400     June 24 Purchases        400
                        ═══                              ═══

                              Bank
                                                          £
                                June 30 BJ Co            500
                                        Factum Ltd       400
```

Numac's payment of £500 to BJ Co appears on the debit side of BJ's Account, reducing the liability to £400. The effect of this can be seen when BJ's Account is balanced. A figure of £400 is carried down to the credit side of BJ's Account at the beginning of July, showing that BJ is still a creditor, but now a creditor for only £400.

Whenever a personal account has a credit balance, it signifies that the person or firm is a **creditor**: hence credit — creditor meaning one to whom a debt is owed.

For Factum Ltd, the payment of £400 completely settles the outstanding debt. At the end of June there is nothing to carry forward. By entering the payment of £400 on the credit side of the account, the debit and credit sides are made equal. Numac no longer owes any money to Factum Ltd.

One must be able not only to produce accounts from given information, but also to explain the full meaning of each entry in an account. Just as, when learning French, one has to translate from English to French and from French to English, so one must be able to translate into and out of the language of accounting.

Consider the following account of A Bennett in the books of Numac:

	A Bennett				
		£			£
July	1 Balance	60	July	3 Bank	50
	12 Sales	80		31 Balance	160
	25 Sales	70			
		210			210
Aug	1 Balance	160			

You may be asked to explain fully the meaning of each entry. The entries can be taken in date order.

On 1 July, Bennett's Account shows a debit balance of £60. This means that Bennett is a debtor to Numac for £60; he owes £60. Two days later, on 3 July, Bennett pays Numac by cheque £50. This is clear because against the figure of £50 is written 'Bank', showing that the corresponding double entry can be found in the Bank Account.

On 12 July Bennett buys £80 of goods from Numac on credit. If this had not been a credit sale, there would have been no entry at all in Bennett's Account.

On 25 July, Numac sells a further £70 of goods on credit to Bennett.

At the end of the month, Bennett's Account is balanced, showing that during the month his indebtedness to Numac increased to £160. This amount is carried to the debit side of Bennett's Account on 1 August, showing that at the beginning of August Bennett is a debtor to Numac for £160.

A similar process of interpretation can be carried out on a creditor's account. G Eliot's Account in the books of Numac is:

	£			£
July 30 Bank	800	July 1	Balance	650
		12	Purchases	150
	800			800

G Eliot

Note that on 1 July Eliot's Account shows a credit balance of £650, showing that Eliot is a creditor to Numac. In other words, Numac owes Eliot £650.

On 12 July, Numac buys goods for resale £150 on credit. Only goods bought for resale are entered in the Purchases Account. Again, if the goods had been paid for, no entry would have been made in Eliot's Account, so the fact that an entry has been made in his Account signifies that the items were purchased on credit.

Finally, on 30 July Numac settles its debt with Eliot by cheque for £800. Thus, the account is balanced, and there is no outstanding figure to carry forward to the following period.

In this type of problem, the key is to discover at the outset whether one is dealing with a debtor or creditor. One can learn this by looking for the opening balance on the account. If it is on the debit side one is likely to be dealing with a debtor; if it is on the credit side one is likely to be dealing with a creditor.

If the account is for a new customer or supplier, there will be no opening balance, so one should look at the closing balance. Again, a debit balance shows a debtor, and a credit balance shows a creditor.

Memo

From Accountant
To   General Manager   *Date* 8.8.19-1

Overdue Debtors

I have been analysing the debtors and notice that
several customers have been owing us some large
sums of money for well over three months despite
the usual reminders. I felt that you should be
made aware of the situation in case you should
wish to stop further supplies.

A F Jones has a debtor balance of £686.74 which is
due mainly to purchases of £135, £142 and £324 for
the last three months. £50 was received in April
in part payment of the outstanding balance. The
outstanding balance at the end of March was £135.74.

M E Barnes has a debtor balance of £647.70. No
money has been received since February although
purchases of £122, £62, £52.70, £64 have been made
for April to July respectively, with an outstanding
balance at the end of March of £347.00.

F C Wallace has a debtor balance of £354 made up
of balance at the end of March of £80.72 and
purchases each month of £57, £82, £37, £97.28 for
April to July inclusive.

Perhaps you will let me know if you wish any
action to be taken.

Tabulation

There are many types of information, other than that appearing in the accounting records, which have to be collected together and presented in a way that highlights the important aspects and makes them easily understandable. Over the years, accounting procedures have established certain conventions, but this is not the case in many other areas of data collection. It is for the presenter to decide on the most appropriate display for his reader. *Effective communication* is the key phrase.

The memo on page 64 was sent by the accountant to the general manager. Do you consider that it communicates information effectively?

This is a simple example, but it would have been so much easier to understand if the information had been presented as a table. There is no one right way to present a table of data, but on page 66 is a suggestion; you may like to consider alternative ways of laying out the information.

All the information in the table is referred to as *primary* i.e. it describes the situation from which it is drawn. In this case, it is information drawn from the debtors' accounts for the purpose of displaying their state of indebtedness. *Secondary* data, on the other hand, is abstracted from primary data which has been compiled for some other purpose, or where, perhaps, further calculations will have been made on the primary statistics.

Summary

On completion of this unit plus practice at the exercises you should be able to:

1 Record credit sales and credit purchases from information supplied.
2 Explain the significance of the various entries on a debtor's and a creditor's account.

Unit of measurement

Overdue debtors ←——— *Heading*

	Debtor balance 31.3.19-1 £	April £	May £	June £	July £	Debtor balance 31.7.19-1 £
M E Barnes — Sales to	347.00	122.00	62.00	52.70	64.00	647.70
M E Barnes — Receipts from	-	Nil	Nil	Nil	Nil	-
A F Jones — Sales to	135.74	Nil	135.00	142.00	324.00	686.74
A F Jones — Receipts from	-	50.00	Nil	Nil	Nil	-
F C Wallace — Sales to	80.72	57.00	82.00	37.00	97.28	354.00
F C Wallace — Receipts from	-	Nil	Nil	Nil	Nil	-

Source: Accountant

Double rulling to assist in high-lighting important figures

Decide on objective in drawing table.
Decide whether it is easier to read from left to right or top to bottom

Try to avoid empty spaces.
Make it clear to reader if information is not available by putting a dash or entering N.A. where not appropriate

Exercises

1 Numac made the following sales on credit during May. Enter the transactions in the necessary accounts, and balance the accounts at the end of the month.

May 2   Goods to R White   £30
     7   Goods to J Thoms   £85
     12 Goods to H Prosser   £22
     15 Goods to R White   £50
     22 Goods to H Prosser   £18
     27 Goods to J Thoms   £25

2 During June, Numac purchased for resale the following items on credit. Enter the transactions in the appropriate accounts, and balance the accounts at the end of the month.

June 5   Six crates of paint at £5.40 per crate from K Ball
     10   Forty drums of cleaning fluid from J James at £1.20 per drum
     12   Five loads of sand at £30 per load from K Ball
     16   General items from C Cook valued at £78
     23   Eighteen boxes of disinfectant from C Cook at £2.70 per box
     28   Twenty-five cases of assorted screws at £5.60 per case from K Ball

3 The following items were sold on credit during July. Enter the transactions in the proper accounts, and balance the accounts at the end of the month.

July 9   To I Dalwood – forty eight fencing panels at £3.70 per panel
     11   To S Hobbs – seventy metres of sawn timber at 80p per metre
     13   To S Bush – thirty sacks of cement at £2.30 per sack
     19   To I Dalwood – fourteen metres of piping at £1.05 per metre
     25   To S Bush – fifty two paving slabs at £1.26 each
     29   To S Hobbs – ten litres of paint at £5.75 per litre

4   Enter the following credit purchases in the relevant accounts, and balance the accounts at the end of August.

Aug 3   From Plastrio − 150 garden gnomes at £1.20 each
      9   From Heath's Quarries − nine tonnes of stone at £4.50 per tonne
     14   From Pipe Supplies − twelve boxes of pipe fittings at £30 per box
     21   From Heath's Quarries − five tonnes of stone at £4.50 per tonne
     25   From Plastrio − twenty water butts at £3.60 each
     29   From Pipe Supplies − sixty metres of piping at 78p per m

5   Produce the account of D Downs as it should appear in the books of Numac Co, and balance the account at the end of April.

Apl 12   Downs purchased on credit goods from Numac £40
     18   Numac sold further goods to Downs on credit £70
     24   Downs purchased £80 of goods on credit from Numac
     30   Downs paid Numac £100 cash

6   Use the following information to show the account of Nasty Plant in Numac's books, and balance the account at the end of May.

May 8   Numac bought items from Nasty Plant on credit £160
     19   Nasty Plant sold on credit £50 worth of goods to Numac
     27   Numac purchased further items on credit from Nasty Plant £190
     31   Numac paid Nasty Plant £240 by cheque

7   The following is AB Trading Co's Account in the books of Numac. Explain fully the meaning of each entry.

A B TRADING CO			
	£		£
Jan 1 Balance	200	Jan 5 Bank	200
3 Sales	150	31 Balance	350
19 Sales	200		
	550		550
Feb 1 Balance	350		

8   Explain fully the significance of each entry on the account of P Wood as it appears in Numac's books:

	P WOOD		
	£		£
Feb 6 Bank	500	Feb 1 Balance	600
28 Balance	700	14 Purchases	270
		28 Purchases	330
	1 200		1 200
		Mar 1 Balance	700

9   Record the following transactions in the books of Dillen, a trader. Balance the accounts, and prepare a Trial Balance as at 30 September.

Sept 1   Began business with £12 000 in the bank
      2   Bought by cheque equipment £1400 and stocks £800
      5   Sold goods on credit to: C Munro £44, D Castle £57, E Matthews £115
      7   Cash sales £77; paid by cheque for rent £80, and for heating oil £210
      10 Purchased stock items on credit from: J Berry £362, D Coy £141, W Murphy £223
      12 Cash sales £92; transferred from bank account to Cash Account £200
      13 Cash sales £147; paid by cash rent £80 and wages £50
      17 Sold goods on credit to D Castle £73, E Matthews £85, C Munroe £76
      20 Cash sales £152; paid rent by cheque £80, and wages by cash £50
      23 Purchased stocks on credit from D Coy £79, J Berry £118, W Murphy £137
      28 Paid cash for postage £10, petrol £17 and rent £80
      29 D Castle paid £80 and C Munro £120, both by cheque
      30 Paid by cheque J Berry £400, D Coy £220, W Murphy £300

10   Record the following in the accounts of C Down, a trader. Balance the accounts, and extract a Trial Balance as at 31 March.

Mar 1 Began business with £26000 cash
    2 Transferred £24000 cash to a business bank account and purchased premises by cheque £15000
    3 Bought fixtures and fittings £2200 on credit from Equipu
    8 Bought goods on credit from A Eliot £420, J Bavy £176, P Archer £282
    9 Cash sales £111; received rent from tenant of garage £20 by cheque
    14 Sold goods on credit to D Williams £37, A Ellis £112, M Ware £91
    16 Cash sales £185; rent received £20 cash
    17 Paid expenses by cash: telephone £64, electricity £42, cleaning £24
    22 Bought goods on credit: A Eliot £280, P Archer £188, J Bavy £214
    24 Cash sales £212
    25 Sold goods on credit to M Ware £29, D Williams £43, A Ellis £98
    28 Paid postage £14 cash; received rent £20 cash
    29 Customers paid by cheque: D Williams £80, A Ellis £170, M Ware £86
    30 Paid suppliers by cheque: A Eliot £500, J Bavy £340, P Archer £270

11　In 1972 the number of trade unions was 504 with a membership of 11.350 million, composed of 8.445 million males and 2.905 million females. In 1973 this had increased to 515, but the following years saw the number fall to 501 then 492 and 462 in 1976. The total union membership, on the other hand, shows a steady increase year by year, with 11.448 million in 1973 and 11.775m, 12.184m and 12.376m in 1974, 1975 and 1976 respectively. Male membership fell slightly to 8.443 million in 1973 and then increased 0.0161% in 1974 and then by 0.0165% in 1975, but only by 0.0109% in 1976. Females showed significant increases of 100 000 in 1973, 171 000 in 1974, 286 000 in 1975 but only 98 000 in 1976.

Tabulate the above information to make clear the relative, as well as the absolute, changes which have taken place over five years. Include any secondary statistics you consider relevant. (Objective C1)

12   Tabulate the following information sent as a memo from the accountant to the general manager. (Objective C1)

MEMORANDUM

To   General Manager

From   Accountant   *Date*   26th Oct. 19-1

Subject   Canteen

I have been analysing the canteen accounts and I felt you should be made aware that the canteen last week (week 39) took £172.57 whereas it was £180.32 the week before and £206.36 in week 37. Purchases from local suppliers were £69 last week, £65 for week 38 and £58 for week 37. Salaries are a constant amount at present of £103 each week. You will readily see that the canteen profit is falling rapidly. Perhaps you will let me know if you wish any action to be taken.

---

13   Tabulate the following information, and include any secondary statistics which may assist in describing the pattern of employment in the firm.

The firm employs 3560 people in total, 1970 of these are men, 780 are women and the remainder are termed young people (being under the age of 18 years), $2/3$rds are male and $1/3$rd female. There are three main departments − production, sales and administration. 20% of men and 35% of women over 18 years are employed in the sales department, and 70% of the young people are employed in the factory in the proportion of 6:3 male to female. $33^1/_3$% of women are employed in administration with the remainder in production. Of the remaining males, some 1300 work in production and the remainder in administration. Of the young people, 100 males work in the sales department and the remainder in administration. Exactly the same number of young females work in administration as there are young males in that department, the remainder working in sales.

6 Profits: the Trading and Profit and Loss Account

Previous units have shown the method of keeping accounts in the orthodox double entry manner. The accounts have distinguished between assets and liabilities, income and expenses. However, one of the main reasons for keeping an orthodox set of accounts is to enable profit figures to be reliably and quickly calculated.

Why calculate profit?

Clearly, when someone starts a business, he does so primarily to make profits: to be better off at the end of a trading period than at the beginning.

The firm's owner will wish to know how well his business is doing. He may wish to compare the actual profit earned with what he planned to earn, so that he can analyse the strengths and weaknesses not only of his business, but of the way that he manages that business. He may wish to use the profit figure to forecast the desirability of expansion in particular markets; to help him decide whether or not to continue doing what he has done in the past.

Not only is the proprietor interested in the profit figure; the firm's creditors might also be interested in knowing just how capable the firm is of paying its debts. A prospective purchaser of a business will wish to see profit figures for previous years to learn what the trend has been; so too will a bank manager, or anyone else who might be asked to lend money to the firm. Naturally, the tax authorities will be keen to learn how much profit has been earned and how profits have been calculated, since the amount of tax payable will be influenced by both factors.

How is profit calculated?

If an item is bought for £20 and sold for £30 a profit of £10 has been made. Profit is simply the selling price less the cost price:

Profit = Selling price − Cost price

Not only is this how you and I would calculate profits for our personal transactions; it is how firms calculate their profits, too. Of course, the firm performs the calculation within the framework of double entry accounting and there are other complications, but basically the calculation remains the same.

The profit calculation is conducted in two stages: firstly, a **gross profit** is calculated, and secondly a **net profit**.

The **gross profit** is simply the profit earned by the firm from its trading activities; in other words, the profit earned merely from buying and selling. This profit is calculated in the Trading Account.

The second step is to calculate the **net profit**. This is the gross profit less the firm's running expenses. Net profit is calculated in the Profit and Loss Account.

Gross profit = Sales − Purchases

Net profit = Gross profit − Running expenses

This could be shown in diagramatic form as a **component bar chart** i.e. each of the bars is subdivided into its component parts (see page 74).

The Trading Account

The purpose of the Trading Account is to calculate the firm's gross profit. To do this, it must bring together figures for both sales and purchases.

Assume that Numac's sales for the period amounted to £65 000, whilst £35 000 had been spent on purchases. The gross profit for the period would be £30 000.

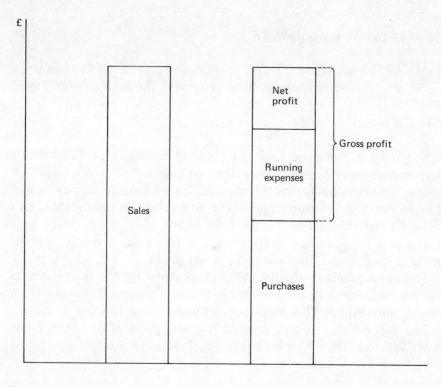

Component bar chart

Now use a Trading Account to calculate the gross profit. In the ledger, the Purchases Account will show a balance on the debit side of £35 000 and the Sales Account will show a credit balance of £65 000.

Purchases		Sales	
£			£
Balance 35 000		Balance	65 000

Each of these figures is transferred to the Trading Account and the accounts for Purchases and for Sales are closed. Remember, each transaction must be entered once on the debit side and once on the credit side. The purchases figure is transferred by crediting the

Purchases Account, with £35 000 — and thus closing the account — and debiting the Trading Account.

The sales figure is transferred by debiting the Sales Account with £65 000 — and thus closing the Sales Account — and crediting the Trading Account.

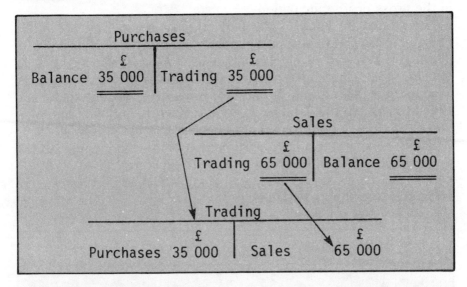

It can now be seen that in order to make the debit side of the Trading Account equal to the credit side, it is necessary to add £30 000 to the debit side. This £30 000 is the gross profit. The gross profit will always be shown as an entry on the debit side of the Trading Account. It will be the amount necessary to balance the account.

	Trading		
	£		£
Purchases	35 000	Sales	65 000
Gross profit	*30 000*		
	65 000		65 000

Stocks

In most cases, a firm will begin an accounting period with stocks in hand; it will also have unsold items remaining at the end of the period. Valuations for each of these stocks will have to be included in the gross profit calculation.

The stocks on hand at the beginning of the period are often referred to as **opening stocks**, while the stocks on hand at the end of a period are referred to as **closing stocks**. In the Trading Account, opening stocks are added to purchases to show the value of goods available for sale during the period. Similarly, closing stocks are added to sales in the Trading Account. Thus, the implicit assumption is that the goods have either been sold or are still in stock.

Using the above example, assume that Numac's opening stocks were valued at £5200, while the closing stocks were valued at £6000. Follow the rule as stated, adding opening stocks to purchases, and adding closing stocks to sales:

Trading				
	£			£
Opening stock	5 200	Sales		65 000
Add Purchases	35 000	*Add Closing stock*		6 000
	40 200			
Gross profit	30 800			
	71 000			71 000

By including the stock figures, the gross profit — which is still the balance in the Trading Account — increases from £30 000 to £30 800. £800 is the difference between the opening and closing stocks.

It should be clear that any *increases* in the opening stock figure will *reduce* gross profit, whilst an *increase* in closing stock will *increase* gross profit. Find what happens if the opening stock in the above example is increased by £300, and redraft the Trading Account. Then repeat the exercise by increasing the closing stock by £300.

Increases in opening stock
      or   } Reduces gross profit
Decreases in closing stock

Decreases in opening stock
      or   } Increases gross profit
Increases in closing stock

The figure for stocks is usually calculated by **stocktaking**. That is, the number of different items on hand are physically counted and a value put against them; in this way the total value of the stocks on hand can be estimated.

In the ledger itself, there will clearly be a need for a Stock Account to accommodate these figures and to provide the double entries for the figures shown in the Trading Account.

Goods on hand are assets, things owned by the firm. As such, the balance on the Stock Account will be a debit balance. So, before the Trading Account is produced, the Stock Account in Numac's books would appear as:

Stock		
	£	
Balance	5 200	

This figure represents the value of the stocks on hand at the beginning of the accounting period. As such, the £5200 is transferred to the Trading Account as the opening stock figure, and the Stock Account is closed.

Stock			
	£		£
Balance	5 200	*Trading*	5 200

Trading			
	£		£
Opening stock	*5 200*	Sales	65 000
Add Purchases	35 000	*Add* Closing stock	6 000
	40 200		
Gross profit	30 800		
	71 000		71 000

The stock on hand at the end of the period appears on the credit side of the Trading Account, so the double entry for this figure must appear on the debit side of the Stock Account.

Stock			
	£		£
Balance	5 200	Trading	5 200
Trading	*6 000*		

Trading			
	£		£
Opening stock	5 200	Sales	65 000
Purchases	35 000	*Add Closing stock*	*6 000*
	40 200		
Gross profit	30 800		
	71 000		71 000

When, at the end of the period, the Stock Account is balanced, it will show a debit balance of £6000.

So the position is similar to that on pages 48—50 in that the closing stock for one period becomes the opening stock for the next. Whatever goods are in the store at midnight on 31 December — the end of one period — are likely still to be in store at two minutes past midnight on the morning of 1 January — the beginning of the next period.

	Stock		
	£		£
Balance	5 200	Trading	5 200
Trading	6 000	*Balance*	*6 000*
Balance	*6 000*		

The Stock Account is thus rather odd, in that it comes to life only at the end of an accounting period. Additions to stocks are recorded in the Purchases Account, and reductions in stocks are generally recorded in the Sales Account.

Profit and Loss Account

The Profit and Loss Account is used to calculate the net profit. The gross profit is transferred from the debit side of the Trading Account to the credit side of the Profit and Loss Account. Then all running expenses are transferred to the debit side of the Profit and Loss Account, and the expense accounts are closed.

Suppose that when Numac earned the gross profit of £30 800, it incurred running expenses of rent and rates £3000, wages £12 000, and heating £2800. Each of these accounts in the ledger would show debit balances because they are each expense accounts.

	Rent & Rates	
	£	
Balance	3 000	

	Wages	
	£	
Balance	12 000	

	Heating	
	£	
Balance	2 800	

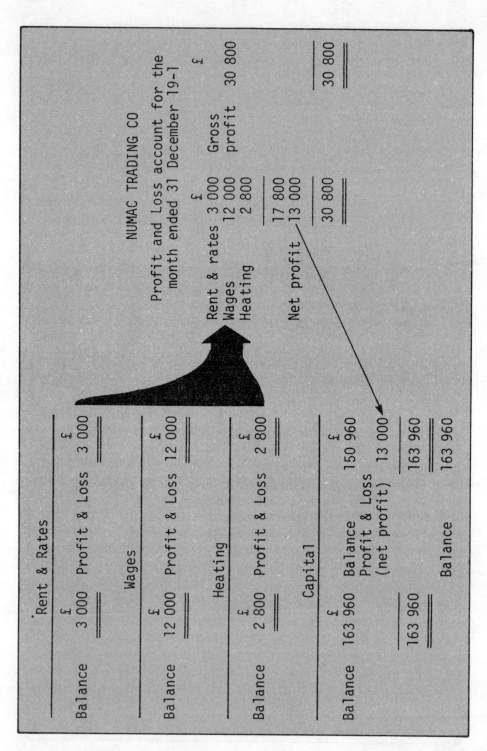

Rent & Rates

	£		£
Balance	3 000	Profit & Loss	3 000

Wages

	£		£
Balance	12 000	Profit & Loss	12 000

Heating

	£		£
Balance	2 800	Profit & Loss	2 800

Capital

	£		£
		Balance	150 960
		Profit & Loss (net profit)	13 000
Balance	163 960		163 960
		Balance	163 960

NUMAC TRADING CO

Profit and Loss account for the month ended 31 December 19-1

	£		£
Rent & rates	3 000	Gross profit	30 800
Wages	12 000		
Heating	2 800		
	17 800		
Net profit	13 000		
	30 800		30 800

In order to transfer these expenses to the Profit and Loss Account, the expense accounts would be credited and closed and the Profit and Loss Account would be debited. Page 80 shows these transactions completed. The expenses to be deducted from the gross profit are listed on the debit side of the Profit and Loss Account.

Now, in order for the Profit and Loss Account to balance, it is necessary to add £13 000 to the debit side. This amount is the net profit. The net profit always appears as an item on the debit side of the Profit and Loss Account.

But where is the double entry for this £13 000? A debit entry has been made in the Profit and Loss Account, but there is no corresponding credit entry. The answer is that the credit entry appears in the proprietor's Capital Account. The profit belongs to him as his reward for setting up the business. When the business earns a profit, the firm's debt to the proprietor is increased by that amount.

C Brown is the proprietor of Numac. Assume that at the beginning of the period his Capital Account had a credit balance of £150 960. The effect of the net profit is to increase this by £13 000. Entering the net profit on the credit side of the Capital Account does increase the credit balance on the Capital Account; in other words, it increases the indebtedness of the firm to the proprietor.

C BROWN
Capital

	£		£
Balance	163 960	Balance	150 960
		Profit & loss	
		(net profit)	*13 000*
	163 960		163 960
		Balance	163 960

Composite accounts

Usually, the Trading and Profit and Loss Accounts are prefaced by a composite heading: Trading and Profit and Loss Accounts . . . Now that each of these accounts has been looked at separately, this composite heading will be used for all future work.

Trading and Profit and Loss Accounts calculate the profits earned over a specified period – a month, six months or a year – and so this must be shown clearly in the heading.

If the above example covered the month ending 31 December 19–1, then the heading and the accounts would be presented as shown below. This is the presentation which will be used in future units for all Trading, and Profit and Loss Accounts. One can always identify the Profit and Loss Account, since it begins with the gross profit on the credit side.

NUMAC TRADING CO

Trading and Profit and Loss Account
for the month ended 31 December 19-1

	£		£
Opening stock	5 200	Sales	65 000
Add Purchases	35 000	*Add* Closing stock	6 000
	40 200		
Gross profit	30 800		
	71 000		71 000
Rent & rates	3 000	Gross profit	30 800
Wages	12 000		
Heating	2 800		
	17 800		
Net profit	13 000		
	30 800		30 800

Cost of goods sold

The usefulness of the Trading Account can be increased, if the figures on it are so arranged as to show the cost of those goods actually sold. Remember that profit is calculated by deducting the cost price from the selling price.

This extra piece of information can be shown quite easily if the closing stock is *deducted* from the debit side of the Trading Account, instead of being *added* to the credit side. Numac's Trading Account after this alteration would then appear as:

```
                        NUMAC TRADING CO

              Trading Account for the month ended
                      31 December 19-1
                          £                               £
Opening stock          5 200      Sales               65 000
Add Purchases         35 000

                      40 200
Less Closing
     stock             6 000

Cost of goods
sold                  34 200
Gross profit          30 800

                      65 000                           65 000
                      ======                           ======
                                  Gross profit         30 800
```

Note that although the *total* of the account is different after this manipulation, the gross profit figure remains unaltered at £30 800.

The Cost of goods sold figure of £34 200 indicates that the items which Numac sold in December for £65 000, actually cost the firm £34 200 to buy. The profit on these sales is thus the difference between the cost price and the selling price:

£65 000 − £34 200   = £30 800
Sales − Cost of goods = Gross profit
         sold

The presentation of the Profit and Loss Account is, of course, unaffected by the change of presentation in the Trading Account.

Losses

It is extremely unlikely that a firm's Trading Account will reveal a gross loss, since this would indicate that the firm had sold items at prices well below what it had paid for them. Note, too, that the firm's overall loss would be greater than just the gross loss, since in the Profit and Loss Account the running expenses would be included, thus increasing the size of the loss.

Profits always appear as credit balances, so by the same token, losses appear as debit balances. Should Numac's sales for December have been only £32 000, then the firm's Trading Account would have recorded a gross loss as follows:

```
                      NUMAC TRADING CO
            Trading Account for the month ended
                     31 December 19-1
                           £                            £
Opening stock          5 200    Sales              32 000
Add Purchases         35 000    Gross loss          2 200

                      40 200
Less Closing
     stock             6 000

Cost of goods
sold                  34 200

                      34 200                        34 200

Gross loss             2 200
```

The cost of goods sold at £34 200 would be less than the sales revenue of £32 000. The difference of £2200 would be the size of the gross loss. This loss figure would then be brought down to the debit side of the Profit and Loss Account so that the running expenses could be added on.

If gross losses are unusual, net losses are not. Again, net losses appear as debit balances on the Profit and Loss Account.

Referring to the earlier example, assume that Numac had, in fact, made a gross profit of £30 800, but that wages for the month were £26 000. The Profit and Loss Account would record the net loss as follows:

```
                    NUMAC TRADING CO

          Profit and Loss Account for the month ended
                      31 December 19-1

                         £                                £
Rent & rates          3 000      Gross profit        30 800
Wages                26 000      Net loss             1 000
Heating               2 800

                     ───────                         ───────
                     31 800                          31 800
                     ═══════                         ═══════
```

Since a net profit increases the owner's stake in the business and appears on the credit side of the Capital Account, so a net loss reduces the owner's stake and the double entry for the loss appears on the debit side of the Capital Account.

```
                        C BROWN

                        Capital
───────────────────────────────────────────────────────────
                         £                                £
Profit and Loss                  Balance              150 960
(net loss)            1 000
Balance             149 960

                    ───────                          ───────
                    150 960                          150 960
                    ═══════                          ═══════
                                 Balance             149 960
```

The appearance of the net loss on the debit side of Brown's Capital Account reduces the balance to be carried forward to the next period, so his stake in Numac is reduced from £150 960 to £149 960. The difference of £1000 is the net loss.

Example of accounts worked through to Balance Sheet

In order to bring together some of the topics discussed in this and earlier units, provided below is the Trial Balance of the Numac Trading Co for the three months ended 31 March 19−1. From the Trial Balance, the ledger accounts are then opened, and the necessary transfers made to the Trading Account and the Profit and Loss Account. Finally, the Balance Sheet is prepared as at 31 March 19−1.

Notice how the transfers are made from the ledger to the Trading and Profit and Loss Accounts. After these transfers the relevant accounts are closed. Indeed, when the Profit and Loss Account has been prepared, the only accounts still remaining open are those carrying Balance Sheet items.

When the Balance Sheet is prepared, remember that the assets are listed in their order of permanence: the more permanent first, and the least permanent, cash, last.

Creditors are easily distinguished from debtors, since their accounts carry credit balances; debtors' accounts carry debit balances. The total for creditors is thus

£1943 + £2189 + £1998 = £6130

Similarly the debtors' total is:

£4724 + £3863 + £5219 + £2471 + £1983 = £18 260

Note, too, that Drawings appear as a deduction from Capital in the Balance Sheet. Drawings **do not** appear in the Profit and Loss Account.

NUMAC TRADING CO

Trial Balance as at 31 March 19-1

	£	£
Purchases and sales	95 250	135 700
Stock at 1 January 19-1	3 050	
Wages	17 911	
Advertising	2 710	
Postage	434	
Motor expenses	1 863	
Telephone	381	
Premises	87 000	
Equipment	9 000	
Vans	10 740	
Furniture	3 300	
Cash	590	
Bank	4 520	
C Hearn	4 724	
M Williams	3 863	
D Parsons	5 219	
J Smith	2 471	
W Horler	1 983	
Capital		119 099
Drawings	5 920	
Universal Supplies		1 943
Commercial Appliances		2 189
Household Ware Ltd		1 998
	260 929	260 929

Stock on hand 31 March 19-1: £4380

Purchases

		£			£
Mar 31	Balance	95 250	Mar 31	Trading	95 250

Sales

		£			£
Mar 31	Trading	135 700	Mar 31	Balance	135 700

Stock

		£			£
Mar 31	Balance	3 050	Mar 31	Trading	3 050
	Trading	4 380			

Wages

		£			£
Mar 31	Balance	17 911	Mar 31	Profit & Loss	17 911

Advertising

		£			£
Mar 31	Balance	2 710	Mar 31	Profit & Loss	2 710

Postage

		£			£
Mar 31	Balance	434	Mar 31	Profit & Loss	434

Motor Expenses

	£			£
Mar 31 Balance	1 863	Mar 31 Profit & Loss		1 863

Telephone

	£			£
Mar 31 Balance	381	Mar 31 Profit & Loss		381

Premises

	£
Mar 31 Balance	87 000

Equipment

	£
Mar 31 Balance	9 000

Vans

	£
Mar 31 Balance	10 740

Furniture

	£
Mar 31 Balance	3 300

Cash

	£
Mar 31 Balance	590

Bank

	£
Mar 31 Balance	4 520

C Hearn

	£
Mar 31 Balance	4 724

M Williams

	£
Mar 31 Balance	3 863

D Parsons

	£
Mar 31 Balance	5 219

J Smith

	£
Mar 31 Balance	2 471

W Horler

	£
Mar 31 Balance	1 983

Capital

	£
Mar 31 Balance	119 099

Drawings

	£
Mar 31 Balance	5 920

Universal Supplies

	£
Mar 31 Balance	1 943

Commercial Appliances

	£
Mar 31 Balance	2 189

Household Ware Ltd

		£
	Mar 31 Balance	1 998

NUMAC TRADING CO

Trading and Profit & Loss Account
for the three months ended
31 March 19-1

	£		£
Opening stock	3 050	Sales	135 700
Purchases	95 250		
	98 300		
Less Closing stock	4 380		
Cost of goods sold	93 920		
Gross profit	41 780		
	135 700		135 700
Wages	17 911	Gross profit	41 780
Advertising	2 710		
Postage	434		
Motor expenses	1 863		
Telephone	381		
	23 299		
Net profit	18 481		
	41 780		41 780

```
                    NUMAC TRADING CO
           Balance Sheet as at 31 March 19-1
                         £                                    £
Capital              119 099    Fixed assets
Net profit            18 481    Premises               87 000
                     --------   Equipment               9 000
                     137 580    Vans                   10 740
Drawings               5 920    Furniture               3 300
                     --------                          --------
                     131 660                           110 040
Current                         Current assets
liabilities                     Stock      4 380
Creditors              6 130    Debtors   18 260
                                Bank       4 520
                                Cash         590
                                           ------
                                                        27 750
                                                       --------
                     137 790                           137 790
                     ========                          ========
```

Summary

On completion of this unit plus practice at the exercises you should be able to:

1 Produce a simple set of Trading and Profit and Loss Accounts.
2 Explain the effect of profits and losses on capital.
3 Explain the significance of the term 'cost of goods sold'.

Exercises
To meet objective G4

1 Explain the meaning of the following terms:

gross profit	opening stock
net profit	closing stock
cost of goods sold	trading
net loss	drawings

2 What is the purpose of
a the Trading Account and
b the Profit and Loss Account?

3 Why should the Trading Account and the Profit and Loss Account be headed 'for the period ended' a certain date?

4 a Produce Trading Accounts from the following information, showing clearly the cost of goods sold.

	Opening stock £	Purchases £	Closing stock £	Sales £
a.	10 000	40 000	9 000	71 000
b.	7 600	37 500	8 100	67 500
c.	4 850	29 220	4 520	49 550
d.	12 740	59 630	13 480	98 890

b Repeat 4a assuming that in each case the value of opening stocks is increased by £400.
c Repeat 4a assuming that in each case the value of closing stocks is increased by £400.

5 Produce Profit and Loss Accounts from the following details:

	a	b	c	d	e
Gross profit	21 000	38 400	45 220	19 380	24 780
Wages	12 000	15 920	19 360	14 560	18 310
Lighting	500	790	850	1 530	1 320
Rent	970	2 600	3 740	2 580	4 640
General expenses	1 430	690	1 050	1 330	1 730

6 Explain the significance of each entry in the following account:

Stock			
Year 1	£	Year 1	£
Jan 1 Balance	7 900	Dec 31 Trading	7 900
Year 2			
Jan 1 Trading	8 300		

7 In each of the following you are required to:
a Open the Sales, Purchases and Stock Accounts
b Transfer the balances to the Trading Account
c Complete the Trading Account to show the gross profit.

	Sales	Purchases	Stocks	
			Opening	Closing
	£	£	£	£
a.	177 500	100 000	25 000	22 500
b.	135 000	75 000	15 200	16 200
c.	148 650	87 660	14 550	13 560
d.	395 560	280 520	50 960	53 920

8 Explain the significance of each entry in the following accounts:

Capital

		£			£
Dec 31	Drawings	4 300	Jan 1	Balance	12 700
	Balance	14 900	Dec 31	Profit &	
				Loss	6 500
		19 200			19 200
			Jan 1	Balance	14 900

Capital

		£			£
Dec 31	Drawings	6 700	Jan 1	Balance	14 000
	Profit &				
	Loss	8 400	Dec 31	Balance	1 100
		15 100			15 100
Jan 1	Balance	1 100			

9 From the following Trial Balance of C Thompson, you are required to draw up Trading and Profit and Loss Accounts for the year ended 31 December 19−2, and a Balance Sheet as at that date. You should also show C Thompson's Capital Account as it would appear at 31 December 19−2.

```
        Trial Balance as at 31 December 19-2
                                          £         £
Capital  B                                       23 560
Stock at 1 Jan 19-2                       8 123
Sales                                             46 155
Purchases                                28 450
General expenses                            263
Advertising                                 277
Rates and insurance                       1 675
Motor expenses                            1 300
Salaries                                  5 375
Premises                                 13 750
Vehicles                                  3 000
Debtors                                   4 875
Creditors                                          3 845
Cash at bank                              4 134
Cash in hand                                100
Drawings                                  2 238
                                         ───────   ───────
                                         73 560    73 560
                                         ═══════   ═══════
Stock at 31 December 19-2: £6370
```

10 From the following Trial Balance of R Oakes you are required to prepare:
a Trading and Profit and Loss Accounts for the year ended 31 March 19-3
b A Balance Sheet at that date
c Oakes' Capital Account as at 31 March 19-3.

```
     Trial Balance of R Oakes as at 31 March 19-3

                                      £            £
Purchases and sales ⊤            74 900      80 800
Rent and rates P+L                2 989
Light and heat P+L                1 477
Stock at 1 April 19-2 ⊤           8 313
Wages and salaries P             11 074
Insurance P+L                       492
Premises B                      155 000
Fixtures B                        3 500
General expenses P-L              1 770
Debtors and creditors B          11 080       4 221
Cash at bank B                   13 460
Drawings B                        8 400
Delivery vans B                  19 250
Vehicle expenses P+L              3 966
Capital B                                   230 650

                                315 671     315 671

Stock at 31 March 19-3: £14 580
```

Note: the questions following Unit 7 provide further practice, if it is desired to present them in a horizontal manner.

Assignment 1

To meet Objectives C1, G1, G2, G4

C Brown decided to form a second business called Brown Electrics. He had found that customers who purchased electrical items from him often wished him to instal or to service the appliances.

Brown began his second business with £2000 in a business bank account and a second-hand van valued at £840. He employed one service engineer at a salary of £60 per week. Brown Electrics used a workshop attached to Numac Trading Co's buildings, for which the electrical company was to pay rent to Numac. Numac also did much of the clerical and administrative work for Brown Electrics.

a From the information given below you are required to produce an orthodox set of accounts for Brown Electrics for the firm's first full month of operation. Balance the accounts at the end of the month, draft a Trial Balance, and produce Trading and Profit and Loss Accounts for the month and a Balance Sheet as at 28 April 19−1.

All servicing was done on a cash with order basis. The following summary of cash receipts for April was extracted from the service engineer's pocket book.

Day	£	Day	£	Day	£	Day	£
3	—	10	27	17	27	24	27
4	—	11	37	18	31	25	42
5	36	12	46	19	59	26	55
6	23	13	68	20	64	27	74
7	49	14	83	21	125	28	136

April 3 Began the business with £2000 in a business bank account, and a second-hand van valued at £840

4 Purchased various items of equipment on credit from Electrical Supplies Ltd £747, two thirds of these were to be used within the new business and the remaining items were spare parts taken into stock for resale

5 Paid road tax and insurance by cheque £176
6 Paid wages by cheque £60
7 Paid rent for workshop to Numac £20
10 Paid postage by cash £2.40
11 Bought stock items on credit from Whites Appliances Ltd £74; paid £21 by cheque for stationery
12 Paid by cheque for telephone installation £40
13 Paid wages by cash £60
14 Paid the following by cash: window cleaner £2.70, office cleaner £10; paid rent to Numac by cheque £20; paid all but £40 cash into bank
17 Bought stock items on credit from Whites Appliances Ltd £116 and from Electrical Supplies Ltd £33
18 Bought spare parts on credit from Lotus Home Services Ltd £87
19 Paid Numac for share of heating oil by cheque £84
20 Paid cash for wages £60 and postage £3.60
21 Paid rent by cheque to Numac £20; paid office cleaner by cash £10; paid all but £30 cash into the bank
24 Withdrew £100 from the bank for private purposes
25 Paid insurance for workshop by cheque £68 and paid petrol bill for month, cash £32
26 Bought further items from Whites Appliances Ltd £26 on credit; took goods valued at £20 for own use
27 Paid wages by cash £60 and repair bill for van, cash £21
28 Paid office cleaner £10 cash, and Numac's rent £20 by cheque; paid off all outstanding debts by cheque; paid all cash into bank except £32 withdrawn for own use and £30 remaining as float.

b During the year Brown Electrics built a double garage on the site. Since the firm had only one van, the garage was rented out.

The list of balances for the firm as at 31 March 19–2 is given opposite. From it you are required to produce the firm's Trading and Profit and Loss Account for the year ended 31 March 19–2 and a Balance Sheet as at that date.

BROWN ELECTRICS

List of balances as at 31 March 19-2

	£
Capital	2 840
Garage	1 730
Van	840
Equipment in workshop	498
Wages	3 120
Rent paid to Numac	1 040
Petrol and van repairs	464
Road tax and insurance	176
Workshop insurance	204
Postage	71
Carriage in	125
Telephone	197
Window cleaner	33
Office cleaner	500
Lighting and heating	482
Administration expenses	892
Rent from garage tenant	374
Creditors	2 163
Purchases	9 945
Income from servicing	18 308
Cash at bank	1 159
Cash in hand	62
Drawings	2 147

Stocks on hand at 31 March 19-2:
£1 170

7 Profits: alternative presentations of information

Unit 6 showed how a Trading Account was used to calculate the gross profit, and how the Profit and Loss Account was used to calculate the net profit. In each case the traditional horizontal presentation was used; the debit entries were written alongside the credit entries.

However, in modern practice, Trading and Profit and Loss Accounts tend to be presented in a vertical manner whereby the figures are listed one under another. There are a number of variations of this approach, but to simplify matters only one such presentation will be explained.

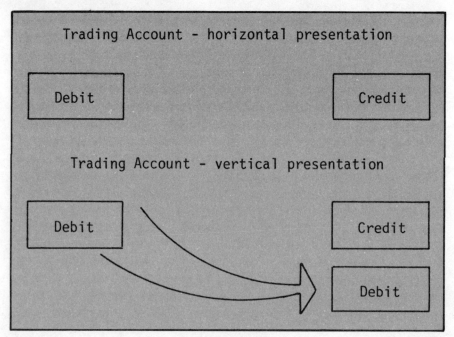

NUMAC TRADING CO
Trading Account - alternative presentations

	£		£
Opening stock	5 200	Sales	65 000
Purchases	35 000		
	40 200		
Closing stock	6 000		
Cost of goods sold	34 200		
Gross profit	30 800		
	65 000		65 000

Figure 3a Horizontal presentation

	£	£	£
Sales			65 000
Opening stock	5 200		
Purchases	35 000		
		40 200	
Closing stock		6 000	
Cost of goods sold			34 200
Gross profit			30 800
			65 000

Figure 3b Vertical presentation

	£	£	£
Sales			65 000
Less Opening stock	5 200		
Purchases	35 000		
		40 200	
Less Closing stock		6 000	
Cost of goods sold			34 200
Gross profit			30 800

Figure 3c Vertical presentation

NUMAC TRADING CO

Profit & Loss Account - alternative presentations

	£		£
Rent & Rates	3 000	Gross profit	30 800
Wages	12 000		
Heating	2 800		
	17 800		
Net profit	13 000		
	30 800		30 800

Figure 4a Horizontal presentation

	£	£
Gross profit		30 800
Rent & rates	3 000	
Wages	12 000	
Heating	2 800	
		17 800
Net profit		13 000
		30 800

Figure 4b Vertical presentation

	£	£
Gross profit		30 800
Less Rent & rates	3 000	
Wages	12 000	
Heating	2 800	
		17 800
Net profit		13 000

Figure 4c Vertical presentation

NUMAC TRADING CO

Trading Account for six months July to December 19-1

	July £	Aug £	Sept £	Oct £	Nov £	Dec £
Opening stocks	7 000	5 300	4 500	3 800	4 500	5 200
Net purchases	32 300	37 600	40 000	41 300	39 000	35 000
	39 300	42 900	44 500	45 100	43 500	40 200
Less Closing stock	5 300	4 500	3 800	4 500	5 200	6 000
Cost of goods sold	34 000	38 400	40 700	40 600	38 300	34 200
Gross profit	27 400	28 700	31 300	35 300	31 700	30 800
	61 400	67 100	72 000	75 900	70 000	65 000

	July £	Aug £	Sept £	Oct £	Nov £	Dec £
Net sales	61 400	67 100	72 000	75 900	70 000	65 000
	61 400	67 100	72 000	75 900	70 000	65 000

NB Net sales is sales less goods returned to Numac by customers.

Net purchases is purchases less goods returned by Numac to suppliers.

Fig. 3 example a on page 101 shows the horizontal presentation with the debit and credit entries written side by side. This can be converted into a vertical presentation quite easily if the debit items are written under the credit ones. The basic double entry pattern is still discernible in the approach. See example b.

Alternatively, the whole statement can be written in the form of a calculation – example c. Although elements of the horizontal Trading Account can still be seen, double entry principles have been disregarded. However, such vertical accounts may be easier to read, especially for non-accountants.

Similarly, the Profit and Loss Account may be presented vertically. Fig. 4 on page 102 shows Numac's Profit and Loss Account using the horizontal approach, a, the double entry approach presented in a vertical manner, b, and the Profit and Loss Account in the form of a vertically presented calculation, c.

These various presentations satisfy certain accounting conventions, and make clear certain statistical and financial information to the manager who is not a statistician or accountant.

The account on page 103 shows Numac's trading figures for six months from July to December 19−1.

What can be said about these figures? It is possible to see certain trends from the **absolute** figures (the *actual* figures) but very often it is more meaningful to calculate the **relative** change (percentage change), for example, between sales for particular months.

To help a manager recognise quickly the important points of the above table, graphs can be drawn as shown below. Remember: the purpose of a graph is to provide visual impact, so it should be neat, clean and clear to the reader.

Fig. 5 shows sales displayed in a way that makes it easy to see what has been happening during the period July to December. The graph has a number of explanatory points and these should be noted.

It will be seen that the graph mentions **dependent**, (Y-axis vertical line) and **independent** (X-axis horizontal line) variables. The independent variable always goes on the X-axis. How does one decide which is dependent and which is independent? The independent variable is the one that can stand on its own. Thus, Time (e.g. days, months, years) is independent, but Sales are dependent, related to time. Time will always be on the X-axis (the horizontal axis) and Sales will be on the Y-axis (vertical axis). If one were to plot the

Figure 5

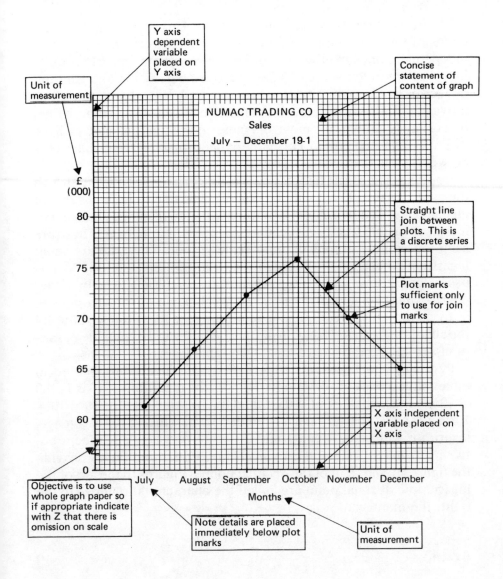

salaries of Numac employees against their years of service, the salaries would be plotted on the Y-axis and the years of service, since it is independent, on the X-axis.

The word **discrete** is used on the graph. Discrete variables are a series of figures which are capable of exact measurement and are independent of each other e.g. the value of sales in October is quite independent of the value of sales in November. Whereas a **continuous** series has a continuity of values e.g. if plotting temperature one moves through each degree to the next, in which case a smooth line, or curve, is drawn. In most business situations the data will be discrete, and one would normally expect to see straight line joins between plots for business graphs.

Looking at absolute figures and plotting these gives one picture, in the case of sales, but it may be equally valuable to look at relative change. This can be achieved by calculating percentage change, but it is also feasible to present relative change in graph form. These are semi-logarithmic graphs or ratio scale graphs. The graph is semi-logarithmic because the X-axis uses a natural scale and the Y-axis uses a logarithmic scale. The presentation can be achieved by either purchasing special logarithmic scale graph paper as shown opposite or by using natural scale paper and plotting the logarithmic values of the absolute figures. Using the latter method will provide the opportunity to revise the use of logarithm tables.

Remember: a logarithm is an index. The logarithms quoted in tables have a base of 10, thus $10 = 10^1$ so the logarithm of 10 is 1; 100 $= 10^2$ so the logarithm of 100 is 2 and for 1000 it is 3 ($10 \times 10 \times 10 = 10^3$) and so on. Therefore, if a number between 10 and 100 is given its logarithm will be between 1 and 2 i.e. all two figure numbers between 10 and 99 will be log 1 something. Logarithm tables provide the figures to the right of the decimal point. (Figures to the left of the logarithmic decimal point are called the characteristic, those to the right, the mantissa.)

Example

To find the logarithm of 77.

77 is between 10 (log 1) and 100 (log 2), therefore its logarithm is $1.-$. The characteristic is 1.

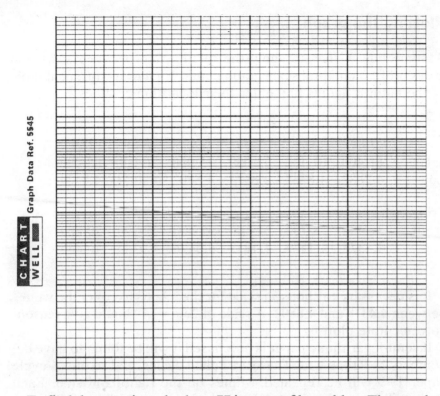

Graph Data Ref. 5545

CHART
WELL ▬▬▬

To find the mantissa, look up 77 in a set of log tables. The number given is 8865. This is the mantissa which follows the characteristic. Thus:

```
no      log
        ch   man
77      1  . 8865
```

When converting logarithmic figures back to natural figures remember that it is only the mantissa which is used. The characteristic indicates where the decimal point will be placed in the natural figure. Thus, if the logarithm of a number is 3.9548, look for the natural value of .9548 in the anti-log table. A value of 9011 will be found. Normally a decimal point would be placed after the first digit, 9.011, but in this case the characteristic is 3, so the decimal is moved 3 places to the right, 9011.0. (If one remembers that the log of 1000 is 3, then obviously any number with a characteristic of 3 must be in the thousands.)

Plotting the graph

Assume one wishes to show the relationship between sales and gross profit on natural scale graph paper. First draw up a neat table of the natural figures and enter their logarithmic values.

	July	Aug	Sept	Oct	Nov	Dec
Sales	61 400	67 100	72 000	75 900	70 000	65 000
Log	4.7882	4.8267	4.8573	4.8802	4.8451	4.8129
Gross profit	27 400	28 700	31 300	35 300	32 700	30 800
Log	4.4378	4.4579	4.4955	4.5478	4.5145	4.4886

It is necessary to choose a scale for the Y-axis to cover the values between 4.4378 and 4.8802. A scale of 2cm = .1 should give reasonably accurate plotting.

If semi-logarithmic paper is purchased it will be found to have the numbers 1−9 repeated. These are called cycles, and so on a 4-cycle paper 1−9 will be repeated 4 times on the right-hand side. Each cycle will be used to plot values which are a multiple of 10 times greater than the previous cycle. For example, the first cycle could represent absolute values 1−9.9, the next cycle 10−99, the next cycle 100−999, and the next 1000−9999. Nevertheless, it is quite acceptable to omit a cycle of numbers if there is no value within that range to plot. The advantage of this graph paper is that the absolute values can be plotted without the need to find logarithmic values.

A semi-log graph shows relative (or percentage) change and so it is the angle of the line not its position which is important. For example, in Fig. 6, compare the angle of the line for sales September to October with the line for gross profit for the same period. The gross profit line is steeper and therefore the percentage increase is greater for gross profit than the percentage increase for sales, so although sales improved, the gross profit improved at a greater rate. The sales line from July to October is nearly a straight line, but on closer inspection it will be noticed that the angle of the line is slightly decreasing. This is confirmed when the percentage increases are calculated. They are 9.28%, 7.30%, 5.41%.

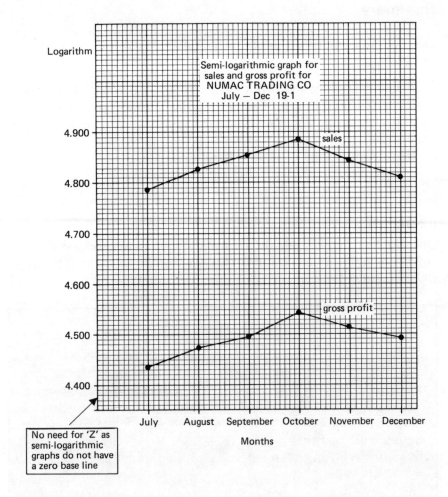

Figure 6

To summarise, a semi-logarithmic graph shows relative change; it is the angle of the line that provides the information, not its position. It is impossible to measure off intermediate points because the plots are on a logarithmic scale (unless you anti-log plot); each cm on the graph does not equal a certain absolute value; there is no base line. Incidentally, it has a further application because data with different units of measurement can be plotted on the same graph since the scale is logarithmic and there is no need to define the unit of measurement.

Summary

On completion of this unit plus practice at the exercises you should be able to:

1 Prepare Trading and Profit and Loss Accounts in vertical form.
2 Construct and interpret semi-logarithmic scale graphs by using natural scale graph paper and by using semi-logarithmic scale graph paper. (B4)
3 Construct graphs of simple functions. (B3)

Exercises

Questions 1, 2 and 3: use the information given to produce Trading and Profit and Loss Accounts for the six months ended as at the Trial Balance date. Present the accounts in vertical form.

1	BOWIE'S BUTCHERY		
Extract from Trial Balance as at 30 September 19-9			
		£	£
Purchases and sales		30 726	49 847
Stock at 1 April 19-9		8 772	
General expenses		284	
Wages and salaries		5 805	
Heating and lighting		1 809	
Advertising		347	
Stationery		174	
Motor expenses		883	
Insurance and rates		299	
Rent received			974
Stock on hand at 30 September 19-9: £6 879			

```
2                  WASHINGTON HARDWARE
Extract from Trial Balance as at 31 December 19-8

                                    £           £
Stock at 1 July 19-8             5 848
Purchases and sales             20 484      27 232
Motor expenses                     936
Wages and salaries               3 870
Heating and lighting             1 206
Advertising                        200
Miscellaneous expenses             189

Stock on hand at 31 December 19-8: £4 586
```

```
3                    CLARK TRADING CO
   Extract from Trial Balance as at 30 June 19-7

                                    £           £
Purchases and sales             26 174      42 463
Stock at 1 January 19-7          7 473
Rent received                                1 382
Salaries                         4 945
Motor expenses                   1 196
Rent and rates                   1 541
Insurances                         255
General expenses                   242

Stock on hand at 30 June 19-7: £5 860
```

NUMAC TRADING CO

Trading Account for six months January to June 19-1

	Jan £	Feb £	March £	April £	May £	June £		Jan £	Feb £	March £	April £	May £	June £
Opening stock	3 050	4 300	2 400	4 380	5 350	5 000	Sales	35 700	42 500	57 500	47 300	63 000	72 000
Purchases	29 750	27 600	37 900	27 670	38 750	47 300							
	32 800	31 900	40 300	32 050	44 100	52 300							
Less Closing stock	4 300	2 400	4 380	5 350	5 000	7 000							
Cost of goods sold	28 500	29 500	35 920	26 700	39 100	45 300							
Gross profit	7 200	13 000	21 580	20 600	23 900	26 700							
	35 700	42 500	57 500	47 300	63 000	72 000		35 700	42 500	57 500	47 300	63 000	72 000

Numac's Trading Account for the period January to June 19−1 is given opposite.

4 *a* Using the January to June figures, plot a natural scale graph of sales and on the same graph plot purchases.
b Using the January to June figures, plot on a semi-logarithmic scale graph the sales and gross profit.
c From the graphs drawn in answer to *a* and *b*, comment on the information you now have. (Objective B1, B3, B4)

5 Carry out a survey of government publications (Department of Employment Gazette, Department of Trade Journal, Monthly Abstract of Statistics etc.) and see if you can find examples of semi-logarithmic graphs. Select one such graph and write a brief explanation so that a lay reader may understand what the graph shows. Why has the particular graph you have chosen been presented as a semi-logarithmic graph rather than as a natural scale graph? (Objective B4)

6 Prepare four semi-logarithmic graphs from the following information and comment on them. (Objective B4)

	1968	1969	1970	1971	1972	1973	1974	1975	1976	1977
Company A turnover (£m)	291	338	439	446	588	933	1164	1184	1672	1823
Company B turnover (£m)	39	48	71	88	118	209	254	268	319	387
Company A dividend (p)	2.9	3.3	3.6	3.7	4.2	4.5	4.9	5.4	8.0	9.5
Company B dividend (p)	0.4	0.4	0.6	1.0	1.5	1.9	2.0	4.0	4.5	7.0

8 Averages and basic indices

Averages

The year's sales for 19–1 as shown on pages 103 and 112 are reproduced below for January to December respectively.

NUMAC TRADING CO - Sales (£) 19-1

Jan	Feb	Mar	Apl	May	June
35 700	42 500	57 500	47 300	63 000	72 000

July	Aug	Sept	Oct	Nov	Dec
61 400	67 100	72 000	75 900	70 000	65 000

Numac's Sales Manager could well find these sales figures interesting, but to give them any relevance in the overall pattern of sales, he might compare them month by month with, say, sales during 19–0 to detect any trends or changes taking place.

One immediate calculation which could be carried out would be to calculate an average. However, there is more than one average and you should be aware of at least three: the arithmetic mean, the median and the mode.

The **arithmetic mean** is what most people commonly refer to as the average i.e. to add up all the figures and divide by the number of items. The total sales for 19–1 is £729 400. Divide this by the number of items, 12, and the arithmetic mean is £60 783.33.

The **median**, on the other hand, is the middle item of a series when placed in numerical order. The median of the series: 3, 5, 7, 9, 12 is 7 because there are five items and the middle item is 7.

The formula $\dfrac{n + 1}{2}$ gives us the median item. N is the number of terms in the series, so in this case:

$$\frac{n + 1}{2} = \frac{5 + 1}{2} = 3$$

The third item, 7, is the median term.

The sales for the year has 12 numbers, thus, the middle values are item 6 and item 7. These two values will be added together and divided by 2. First place the numbers in numerical order:

35 700, 42 500, 47 300, 57 500, 61 400, 63 000, 65 000, 67 100, 70 000, 72 000, 72 000, 75 900

The values of items 6 and 7 are £63 000 and £65 000. Adding them together and dividing by 2 will give a median of £64 000.

Note that the median value will not change if other figures are changed e.g. if January's sales were £25 700 this would not affect the median, although it would, of course, affect the arithmetic mean.

The **mode** is the value that occurs most often in any series. So in the series 3, 5, 7, 7, 9, 12 the mode will be 7 because 7 appears twice and the other numbers only once. The year's sales show that sales of £72 000 were achieved in two months, so the mode is £72 000. We now have 3 averages for sales for 19−1:

Arithmetic mean   £60 783.3
Median   £64 000
Mode   £72 000

It is necessary, therefore, to be precise when using this word 'average'. Numac's Sales Manager could quite legitimately say the average sale for 19−1 was £72 000, but it is not until the question is asked: which average is being used, that one will be aware which calculation has been used.

There are some situations which make one of the averages much more appropriate than another.

116

For example, if the details of the sales of shoes are taken from Numac's stock record cards, the following statement will be obtained:

Sales Sheet: Men's Shoes.   Week ending 31.1.19-1

Size $7\frac{1}{2}$ 3 pairs   Size $9\frac{1}{2}$ 20 pairs
Size 8   12 pairs   Size 10   18 pairs
Size $8\frac{1}{2}$ 10 pairs   Size 11   3 pairs
Size 9   15 pairs

If one wished to calculate the arithmetic mean it would be necessary to multiply size by number of pairs and to add all these values together, then divide by total number of pairs sold as follows:

Size	Pairs	Size × Pairs	Cum. Frequency
$7^1/_2$	3	22.5	3
8	12	96	15
$8^1/_2$	10	85	25
9	15	135	40
$9^1/_2$	20	190	60
10	18	180	78
11	3	33	81
	81	741.5	

The arithmetic mean is $\dfrac{741.5}{81} = 9.154$

However there is no shoe size 9.154. An answer is produced which is of no help to anyone.

The median point is calculated as $\dfrac{n+1}{2}$ therefore

$$\dfrac{81+1}{2} = 41$$

The 41st item will be size $9^1/_2$ (note cumulative frequency column:

there are 40 pairs of shoes up to and including size 9, so the 41st pair of shoes placed in numerical order will be a size $9^1/_2$). So the median, being the mid-point, at least gives a value which has some meaning.

The mode, being the size which occurs most often, will be size $9^1/_2$ because it has sold 20 pairs (more than any other size). Once again, a value is obtained which is recognisable and certainly, in the retail trade, the mode is probably of more use than the other averages when dealing with stock of varying sizes.

Government statistics for average earnings now give the median so that a single value is used showing what the man in the middle of the earnings scale receives. At one time the arithmetic mean was used, but it was thought to be distorted by extreme values i.e. by some very high earnings which gave the impression that the average worker was receiving more than was actually the case.

The main point is to be wary about the term 'average' and apply it with care and common-sense.

Indices

An index is based upon the principle that at a certain date a value shall be considered to be 100 and then actual changes from that point shall be calculated as a change to that 100.

For example, assume it is necessary to calculate the sales for 19−1 as an index commencing in January. January becomes 100 and

$$\text{February will be } \frac{42\ 500}{35\ 700} \times 100 = 119.05 \ (\frac{\text{Feb sales}}{\text{Jan sales}} \times 100)$$

$$\text{March will be } \frac{57\ 500}{35\ 700} \times 100 = 161.06 \ (\frac{\text{March sales}}{\text{Jan sales}} \times 100)$$

$$\text{April will be } \frac{47\ 300}{35\ 700} \times 100 = 132.49 \ (\frac{\text{Apl sales}}{\text{Jan sales}} \times 100)$$

Note that the base figure is the same in all the calculations i.e. the January figure which it was decided should be the base figure. A % sign is not written after the figure. Also note that the difference between February and March is 119.05 to 161.06 i.e. 42.01 which is not 42.01%. It is referred to as 42.01 points (The actual % increase is 35.29%. Why is this?)

This information can be presented as follows:

Month	Jan	Feb	Mar	April
Sales	35 700	42 500	57 500	47 300
Index	100	119.05	161.06	132.49

The use of index numbers has distinct advantages where different units of measurement are being used. For example, Numac could well be selling dress material by the metre, shoes by pairs, bath towels by number. It could be suggested that their selling price be used as a common unit of measurement, but this may well be distorted by inflation affecting different products at different periods of time. Instead, an index could be produced for each. Numac's stock record data shows the following figures:

		Jan	Feb	March	April
Dress material	(m)	4 000	4 200	4 400	3 800
Shoes	(prs)	300	330	390	400
Bath towels	(no)	57	55	60	80

These are difficult to compare as they stand, but the creation of an index for each will make the data become information.

	Index figure			
	Jan	Feb	March	April
Dress material	100	105	110	95
Shoes	100	110	130	133
Bath towels	100	96	105	140

This could be referred to as a 'volume index figure' because the prices have been ignored. It is quite feasible to take this calculation of an index a stage further by producing an overall index for the company. For ease of calculation, assume that the three items given above represent the total sales of Numac. The index figures of the three items could thus be added and divided by 3 (since there are 3 items). February's figure would be $(105 + 110 + 96) \div 3 = 103^2/_3$.

It may well be that each item is not of equal importance and so **weights** can be given to each according to its relative importance. Suppose the Sales Manager decides that the relative weights of the three items shall be 3, 10 and 2. The calculation will be as follows.

Weighted index figure			
	Index	Weight	Index x Weight
Dress material	105	3	315
Shoes	110	10	1100
Bath towels	96	2	192
		15	1607

All items index $\dfrac{1607}{15} = 107.13$

Government departments produce a large number of index figures to show changes in retail volume and prices. Probably the most well known is the Index of Retail Prices (to be found in detail in the Department of Employment Gazette each month) which attempts to show the changes in prices of goods and services paid for by consumers. It uses a weighting system because it is obvious that a price rise in, say, potatoes is more important than a price rise in, say, candles. Thus the principle of weighting is to apportion importance. This relative importance can then be reflected where an all items index is required.

Summary

On completion of this unit plus practice at the exercises, you should be able to

1 Calculate the arithmetic mean, median and mode from discrete data. (D1)
2 Explain the significance and meaning of the arithmetic mean, median and mode. (D1)
3 Calculate a weighted average. (D2)
4 Calculate a weighted average index. (D2)

Exercises

1 The salaries for the month of September for 10 employees selected at random from Numac's payroll are as follows.

£651.75; £327.50; £202.75; £190.75; £137.50; £190.75; £240.80; £540.50; £185.70; £798.20

Calculate the mean, median and mode. Write a memo to the personnel manager outlining the advantages and disadvantages of each in relation to the above figures as a fair reflection of the salaries paid. These figures will be used as a basis for negotiation with the recognised trade unions. (Objective D1)

2 Using Numac's trading figures for the year 19–1 given on pages 103 and 112 calculate an index for the year for sales. (Objective D2)

3 The annual salary earned by one employee over 10 years with Numac is as follows:

	£		£		£
1969	2200	1973	3000	1977	3750
1970	2300	1974	3000	1978	4200
1971	2500	1975	3250		
1972	2700	1976	3450		

a Create an index for his earnings using 1969 as 100
b The Index of Retail Prices for 1969–78 is 100, 105, 114, 123, 132, 147, 176, 206, 239, 261. Comment upon this employee's salary in relation to the Index of Retail Prices

c If the above salaries were to be plotted on a semi-logarithmic graph with the index calculated in *a* above, give your reasons why the two lines drawn would be either the same (i.e. parallel) or different. (Objectives D2, B4)

4   The sales of certain items of Numac's stock over a three year period are given below. Create an index for each product over the three years and obtain an all items index for each year using the weighting given. Round index numbers to nearest integer.

		1976	*1977*	*1978*	*Weighting*
Sheets polyester single	(no)	1 070	1 380	1 680	9
Sheets polyester double	(no)	960	1 276	1 376	16
Pillowcases polyester	(prs)	4 500	4 800	4 700	12
Sheeting	(m)	11 350	9 750	7 680	12
Towel hand	(no)	3 670	3 890	4 050	10
Towel bath	(no)	1 880	1 796	1 850	6
Towelling	(m)	7 500	6 500	5 250	7

If the weights reflected their financial value, what can be said about the company's sales expressed in financial terms? (Objective D2)

5   The following table gives the premium income written by UK insurance companies from 1972–6. Calculate an index for UK premiums and an index for overseas premiums (1972 = 100). Comment on the figures.

	1972	*1973*	*1974*	*1975*	*1976*
UK premiums (£m)	146	150	177	221	285
Overseas premiums (£m)	122	143	170	187	232

Assume a weighting of 5:4 (UK to overseas) as a measure of profitability and calculate a total premiums index for each year.

Assume the UK rate of inflation from 1972–1976 was 100, 107, 120, 144, 168 and the average rate of overseas inflation from 1972–1976 was 100, 105, 110, 116, 122. What can be said about premium income over the years? (Let inflation be the same as the fall in purchasing power of the £). (Objective D2)

9 Presentation of financial data

In Unit 7 it was explained that Trading and Profit and Loss Accounts could be presented in a vertical as well as in a horizontal form. The same is true with Balance Sheets, which can also be presented in a vertical manner. There are a number of ways of showing vertical Balance Sheets, but only one approach will be adopted in this book.

```
                    NUMAC TRADING CO
            Balance Sheet as at 31 July 19-1

                        £                                    £
Capital          150 960      Fixed assets
Net profit         7 425      Premises            127 000
                 -------      Equipment            10 000
                 158 385      Vans                 12 800
                              Furniture             4 300
                                                  -------
                                                  154 100
Current
liabilities                   Current assets
Creditors         14 230      Stock      5 300
                              Debtors   10 600
                              Bank        2 380
                              Cash          235
                                         ------
                                                   18 515
                 -------                          -------
                 172 615                          172 615
                 =======                          =======
```

Above is Numac Trading Co's Balance Sheet as at 31 July 19−1. It is presented in the horizontal manner which earlier units have used.

The liabilities are listed on the left of the Balance Sheet, whilst the assets appear on the right.

The Balance Sheet conforms to the equation:

Capital + Current Liabilities = Fixed Assets + Current Assets

since;

$$£158\ 385 + £14\ 230 = £154\ 100 + £18\ 515$$
$$£172\ 615 = £172\ 615$$

However, many firms produce their Balance Sheets in a vertical manner. It is thought that such a presentation is easier to follow, and certainly it is easier to arrange on the page.

Page 124 shows Numac's Balance Sheet presented in vertical form. The Balance Sheet opens by listing those assets employed by the business. Fixed assets are listed first followed by current assets. Note, too, that the total of current liabilities is subtracted from the figure for current assets. The Balance Sheet shown conforms to the equation:

Fixed Assets + (Current Assets − Current Liabilities) = Capital

since;

$$£154\ 100 + (£18\ 515 - £14\ 230) = £158\ 385$$
$$£154\ 100 + £4285 = £158\ 385$$

The excess of current assets over current liabilities is known as **working capital**. It is a measure of a firm's ability to pay its short-term debts. More will be said about this in Unit 16, but it is sufficient at this stage to remember that the provision of this information increases the usefulness of the Balance Sheet for the firm's own management and for outsiders who may have an interest in the firm's affairs.

The second part of the Balance Sheet shows how Numac has been financed. In the case of a sole trader, where the capital is provided by the proprietor, the only source of long-term finance will be his capital plus any profits which he has yet to withdraw from the firm.

```
                    NUMAC TRADING CO
          Balance Sheet as at 31 July 19-1

                         £          £          £
Assets employed

Fixed assets
Premises                          127 000
Equipment                          10 000
Vans                               12 800
Furniture                           4 300
                                  ————————
                                                154 100
Current assets
Stock                  5 300
Debtors               10 600
Bank                   2 380
Cash                     235
                      ———————
                                   18 515
Less Current liabilities
Creditors                          14 230
                                  ————————
                                                  4 285
                                                ————————
                                                158 385
                                                ════════


Financed by:
Capital                           150 960
Add Net profit                      7 425
                                  ————————
                                                158 385
                                                ════════
```

It is not always easy to understand and pick out the important features of a large table of figures, especially if they are presented according to certain conventions as is a Balance Sheet. Nevertheless, public limited companies are required to keep their shareholders informed of the financial position of the company and for this reason they produce an Annual Report with the year's accounts. Quite often these are produced in glossy book form including not only the full financial details but further information about the company's activities. The concern here, though, is with the financial details. Since these are often complex and difficult to interpret, companies provide aids to better understanding and examples will be given below. The presentations are taken from annual reports and are therefore examples of how financial information can be presented in diagramatic form; they do not provide a complete picture of that particular company's financial state.

Legal and General Assurance Society in their 1977 accounts used a **bar chart** presentation as shown on pages 126 and 127. A clear picture of the company's activities can quickly be obtained from these charts. Note the comments inserted by the authors to assist the reader in preparing bar charts. The main concern is to assist interpretation, so a clean, clear presentation is essential. A further example is given in Unit 10 page 144.

There are occasions when it seems preferable to bring two series of data together for comparison. In these instances a **multiple bar chart** is very useful. United Biscuits (Holdings) Ltd used a multiple bar chart in their 1977 accounts to compare their growth of profit with dividend as shown on page 128. (A scale has been inserted by the authors). This presentation is interesting in that the figures have been converted into an index with 1973 as 100. This has made a comparison between years easier, especially if one appreciates that in 1977 the profit after tax was £19289 and dividend per share 5.38p. Putting those two figures onto a graph would not have been very revealing.

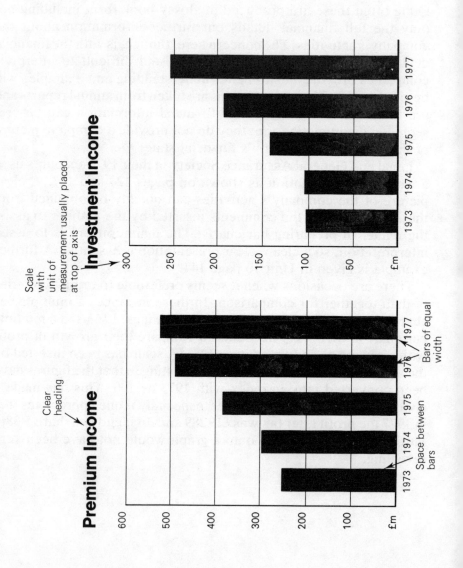

Five Year Review — Legal & General Assurance Society Limited

Premium Income

Clear heading

Space between bars

Bars of equal width

600
500
400
300
200
100
£m

1973 1974 1975 1976 1977

Investment Income

Scale with unit of measurement usually placed at top of axis

300
250
200
150
100
50
£m

1973 1974 1975 1976 1977

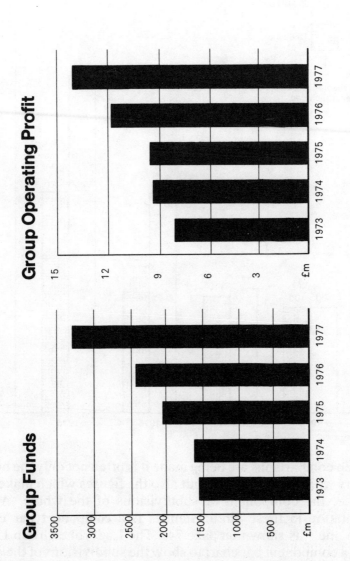

UNITED BISCUIT (HOLDINGS) LTD.

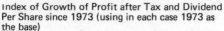

Index of Growth of Profit after Tax and Dividend
Per Share since 1973 (using in each case 1973 as
the base)

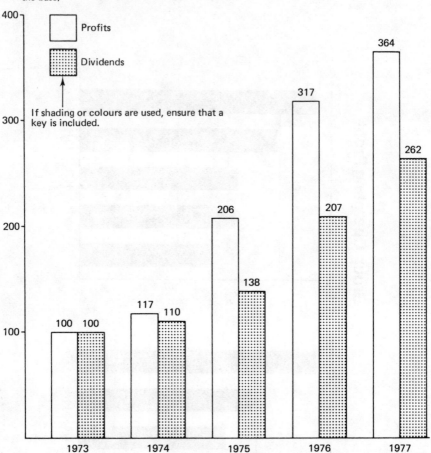

When comparisons are being made it is often not only the height of
the bars which is meaningful but also the figures which make up the
total i.e. the component or subdivisions of the whole. A useful
presentation in these circumstances is a **component bar chart** (a
simple one was shown on page 74). The Ladbroke Group Ltd produced a component bar chart to show the subdivisions of their assets
and liabilities. Obviously these must be equal, so the heights of the
bars for any one year are the same, but what is interesting is the

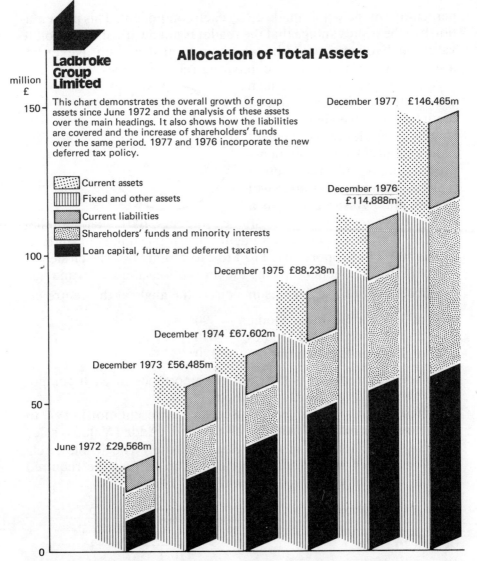

Ladbroke Group Limited

Allocation of Total Assets

million £

This chart demonstrates the overall growth of group assets since June 1972 and the analysis of these assets over the main headings. It also shows how the liabilities are covered and the increase of shareholders' funds over the same period. 1977 and 1976 incorporate the new deferred tax policy.

December 1977   £146.465m

Current assets

Fixed and other assets

Current liabilities

Shareholders' funds and minority interests

Loan capital, future and deferred taxation

December 1976 £114.888m

December 1975 £88.238m

December 1974 £67.602m

December 1973 £56.485m

June 1972 £29.568m

change over the years in the proportion of current to fixed assets and current liabilities to shareholders funds and loan capital. This presentation is shown above.

The component bar chart uses absolute (actual) values but there are occasions when the relative (percentage) values are more meaningful. The **percentage bar chart** meets this need. In this presentation, all the heights of the bars are the same i.e. 100% (the Y- axis scale being 0–100%). The bars will be subdivided according to the percentage of the whole made up by each component. This presentation has the disadvantage that the reader is not aware of the absolute values and so care should be taken not to mislead him. Nevertheless, it is a useful means of comparing relative values.

Another presentation which shows the component parts of the whole is a **pie chart**. This is simply a circle of convenient radius subdivided into segments proportionate to the actual figures. A simple illustration will explain this. Assume that in a 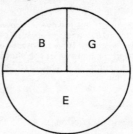 college there are 100 Business Studies students, 100 General Studies students and 200 Engineering students. The total number of students is thus 400. The proportion is 1 to 1 to 2 to a total of 4. The circle will be split into 3 segments showing the proportions i.e. $^1/_4$, $^1/_4$ and $^1/_2$.

Since there are 360 degrees in a circle the angle at the centre is

$^1/_4$ of 360° for Business Studies = 90°
$^1/_4$ of 360° for General Studies = 90°
$^1/_2$ of 360° for Engineering = 180°

Each segment represents the relative importance of each component. The circle represents the whole.

United Biscuits (Holdings) Ltd used such a presentation in 1977 to show how their Added Value was distributed. (Added Value is sales less raw materials and services. See opposite.) The whole circle represents 116.4 million and the calculation to find the required angle at the centre for each segment is as follows:

Benefit to employees	is	$\dfrac{81.4 \times 360}{116.4}$	= 252°
Benefit to state	is	$\dfrac{4.9 \times 360}{116.4}$	= 15°
Benefit to lenders	is	$\dfrac{1.5 \times 360}{116.4}$	= 5°
Benefit to shareholders	is	$\dfrac{4.3 \times 360}{116.4}$	= 13°
Benefit to company	is	$\dfrac{24.3 \times 360}{116.4}$	= 75°
		Total	360°

IN 1977 WE CREATED £116m OF ADDED VALUE

UK sales in 1977 were	**£378m**	**100.0p**
Out of this we had to buy raw materials, fuel and other goods and services which cost	**£262m**	**69.2p**
This left Added Value on UK trading of	**£116m**	**30.8p**

ADDED VALUE PAYS THE WAGES, PROVIDES CASH FOR INVESTMENT IN THE BUSINESS, PAYS TAXES AND PAYS DIVIDENDS TO SHAREHOLDERS AND INTEREST TO BANKS

This is how it was shared out

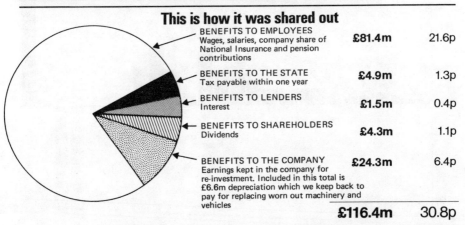

BENEFITS TO EMPLOYEES Wages, salaries, company share of National Insurance and pension contributions	£81.4m	21.6p
BENEFITS TO THE STATE Tax payable within one year	£4.9m	1.3p
BENEFITS TO LENDERS Interest	£1.5m	0.4p
BENEFITS TO SHAREHOLDERS Dividends	£4.3m	1.1p
BENEFITS TO THE COMPANY Earnings kept in the company for re-investment. Included in this total is £6.6m depreciation which we keep back to pay for replacing worn out machinery and vehicles	£24.3m	6.4p
	£116.4m	**30.8p**

HOW UK ADDED VALUE AND UK TRADING PROFIT RECONCILE		
1977 UK Sales		£378.1m
less raw materials etc.		£261.7m
Added Value		£116.4m
less Employee Benefits	£81.4m	
Depreciation	£6.6m	
		£88.0m
Trading profit		£28.4m

Unfortunately, even well run firms have years when losses are made, in which case it is feasible to use the bar chart approach to show this diagrammatically. In the year(s) when losses are made, the bars are drawn below the X-axis using the same scale as for the plus scale. This is well illustrated in the bar chart prepared by the Electricity Council in their Annual Report for 1976/7. (See below)

ELECTRICITY COUNCIL
Consolidated Profit after Interest

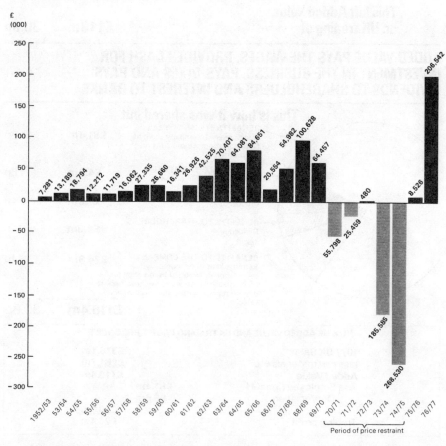

Consolidated profit after interest
£ thousand

6

Below is a **band chart** showing components of the whole in a graphical presentation. It has its limitations because if the components vary widely and cross into another band, the graph will be difficult to understand.

Example of a band chart

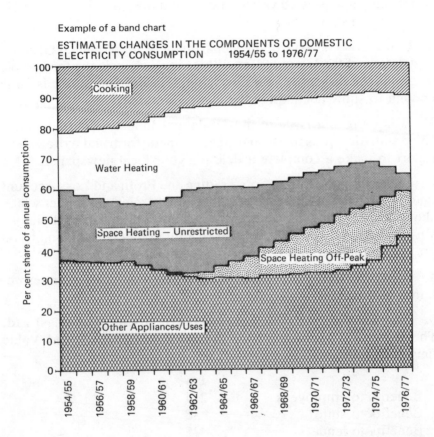

ESTIMATED CHANGES IN THE COMPONENTS OF DOMESTIC ELECTRICITY CONSUMPTION   1954/55 to 1976/77

Summary

On completion of this unit plus practice at the exercises you should be able to:

1 Prepare a simple Balance Sheet in vertical form.
2 Represent data in diagrammatic form and interpret such diagrams. (C2)

Exercises

1   What are the advantages and disadvantages of using pictorial representation? Select from the press examples of pictorial representation which you consider show the advantages, and some which have not assisted you to understand the basic data or may, in fact, have misled you.

2   Using a recent issue of the Department of Employment Gazette, find details of the Index of Retail Prices and show in the form of pie diagrams the last three years' weights. (Ensure your circle is large enough to show adequately the eleven sub divisions)

3   Using a recent issue of the Trade and Industry Journal, select some statistics, present them in diagrammatic form and write a short report to make a complete article for your local newspaper.

4   Using Numac Trading Co's Trading and Profit and Loss Account figures for November and December 19–1, select an aspect which shows a significant change in the two months and display it pictorially so that a non-accountant will readily appreciate the point you are trying to make. (See pages 103 and 112)

5   Using the band chart on page 133, write a report on your interpretation of the diagram.

6   Page 131 shows a pie chart for United Biscuit (Holdings) Ltd. The Bowater Organisation for the same year had Added Value figures as follows:

	£m
Benefits to employees	214
Benefits to state	38
Benefits to lenders	25
Benefits to shareholders	17
Benefits to company	14
	£308

Draw a pie chart using the same radius as used on page 131 and comment upon the two companies.

7   Using the information on Added Value available on page 131 and Question 6, present the two companies' figures in a percentage bar chart. Comment upon this percentage presentation as against the pie chart presentation used in Question 6.

Questions 8–12: in each case you are asked to produce

a Trading and Profit and Loss Accounts in a vertical form for the year
b Balance Sheets as at the year end
c The proprietor's Capital Account at the year end.

8	Trial Balance of J Fisher as at 31 December 19-1		
		£	£
Purchases and sales		34 690	52 986
Stock at 1 Jan 19-1		6 630	
Rent & rates		1 411	
Wages and salaries		10 814	
Insurance		218	
Administrative expenses		605	
Motor expenses		1 860	
Light and heat		465	
Miscellaneous expenses		880	
Premises		14 000	
Vehicles		5 040	
Furniture and fittings		980	
Debtors and creditors		10 910	4 847
Cash at bank		1 350	
Drawings		3 360	
Capital			35 380
		93 213	93 213

Stock at 31 December 19-1: £8249

9   Trial Balance of D Walters as at 31 March 19-4

	£	£
Capital		72 292
Drawings	8 990	
Salaries and wages	14 880	
Advertising	1 930	
Purchases and sales	51 770	79 360
Stock at 1 April 19-3	13 485	
Insurance	465	
Motor expenses	1 916	
General expenses	868	
Rent received		1 614
Premises	46 500	
Vehicles	6 200	
Debtors and creditors	13 392	9 734
Bank	2 604	
	163 000	163 000

Stock at 31 March 19-4: £14 229

10   Trial Balance of E Jones as at 30 September 19-2

	£	£
Capital		41 100
Drawings	6 560	
Purchases and sales	40 180	60 656
Stock at 1 Oct 19-1	12 083	
Salaries and wages	7 830	
Motor expenses	2 125	
Rent	1 460	
Rates	384	
Insurance	467	
Packing expenses	883	
Fuel and power	2 128	
Sundry expenses	368	
Motor vehicles	7 680	
Furniture and fittings	1 920	
Debtors and creditors	14 646	9 744
Cash at bank	12 400	
Cash in hand	386	
	111 500	111 500

Stock at 30 September 19-2: £15 994

11   Trial Balance of W Norris as at 31 December 19-2

	£	£
Purchases and sales	49 155	67 396
Stock at 1 January 19-2	11 990	
Postage and telephone	661	
Salaries	12 656	
Motor expenses	1 157	
General expenses	240	
Rent	1 131	
Rates	450	
Debtors and creditors	13 624	9 205
Premises	29 000	
Motors	6 815	
Furniture	3 248	
Rent received		4 226
Drawings	11 165	
Capital		60 465
	141 292	141 292

Stock at 31 December 19-2: £ 8290

12   Trial Balance of C Hawley as at 31 March 19-5

	£	£
Capital		56 125
Purchases and sales	104 625	117 025
Vehicles	3 045	
Motoring expenses	716	
Land and buildings	17 500	
Bank balance	1 215	
Furniture and equipment	2 285	
Salaries and wages	19 364	
Advertising	2 387	
Rent received		1 832
Drawings	4 400	
Rates and insurance	558	
Cleaning expenses	808	
Debtors and creditors	9 730	9 395
General expenses	3 569	
Stock at 1 April 19-4	14 175	
	184 377	184 377

Stock at 31 March 19-5: £19 800

Assignment 2

(To meet objectives A1, A3, B1, B4, C2, D1, D2)

Assignment 1 provides details of cash receipts for April 19—1 (reproduced opposite). Use these figures to carry out the following analysis. (3 April is a Monday)

1 Calculate the arithmetic mean, median and mode for the month of April and discuss how appropriate each average is to the month's activities.

2 Construct a semi-logarithmic graph to show Week 4 Monday to Friday (24 to 28 April incl.) as one curve, and the total sales on a Monday to Friday basis for the three full weeks as the other curve. Comment on the information conveyed by your presentation.

3 Construct a pie chart for Week 2 and one for Week 3 subdivided into Monday, Tuesday, Wednesday, Thursday, Friday. Use the same radius for each circle. Comment on the information conveyed by your presentation.

4 Select a presentation of your own choice, excluding a pie chart or semi-logarithmic scale graph, with the object of highlighting a significant aspect of April's figures.

5 Calculate an index for each of three full weeks on a Monday to Friday basis, using Monday as the base. If the sales for the first week of May started with an actual cash receipt of £36 and the same rate of increase was expected for the remainder of the week as achieved in the first week of April, calculate the actual receipts. If, on the other hand, the same absolute increase as was achieved on Monday was expected for each day for the remainder of the week, calculate the revised indices.

Day	£	Day	£	Day	£	Day	£
3	—	10	27	17	27	24	27
4	—	11	37	18	31	25	42
5	36	12	46	19	59	26	55
6	23	13	68	20	64	27	74
7	49	14	83	21	125	28	136

10   The Cash Book

Since Unit 3, separate accounts have been kept on separate pages of the ledger to record bank and cash transactions. However, it is more convenient to keep these two accounts in one book of record, known as the Cash Book.

Two versions of the Cash Book will be considered: the two column Cash Book and the similar, but slightly more complicated, three column Cash Book.

Two column Cash Book

The two column Cash Book merely presents the separate Cash and Bank Accounts side by side. The accounts are therefore presented on the same page, but it is important to remember that they remain two separate accounts: they are kept together merely for convenience. The normal practices of double entry also still apply.

Before going on to study the example, look carefully at the way the two column Cash Book is ruled up. (See opposite) From this it should be clear how the two column Cash Book gets its name.

The Cash Book is divided into two sides — debit and credit — but on each side there are two columns. On the debit side of the Cash Book the debit entries are recorded for the Cash Account and the debit entries for the Bank Account. Similarly on the credit side; the ·credit entries are recorded for the Cash Account and the credit entries for the Bank Account.

To see how the two column Cash Book operates, the following example is produced in both presentations:

October 1   Money in the bank £1900; cash in till £84; cash sales £160

2   Paid for purchases by cash £180; paid window cleaner £4 cash; cash sales £140

3   Customers paid by cheque: J Taylor £76, G Williams £57; cash sales £130

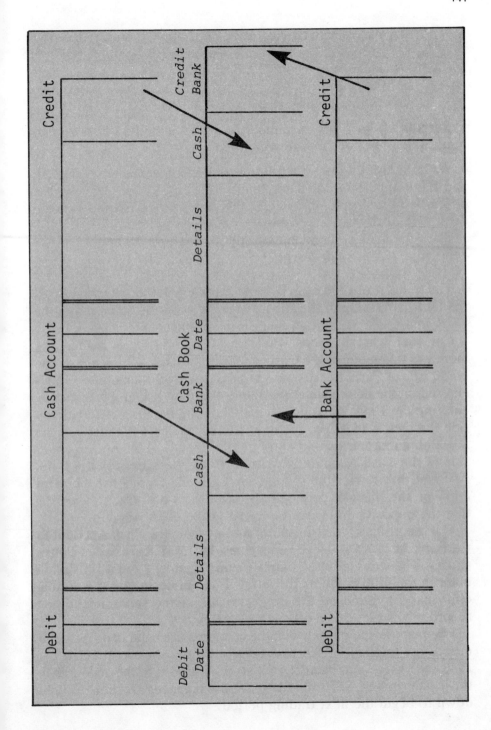

4   Wages paid by cash £56; paid suppliers by cheque: R T Ltd £400, Em Co £320; customer R Constable paid his account by cash £36; cash sales £190

5   Paid petrol bill by cheque £23; cash sales £250; paid £700 into bank

Carefully follow this example through each method of presentation, taking note of the following points:

a With the two column Cash Book, the opening balances for Cash and Bank appear on the same line.

b The debit cash column contains the same entries as appear on the debit side of the Cash Account.

c The debit bank column contains the same entries as appear on the debit side of the Bank Account.

The transfer of £700 from Cash to Bank on October 5 emphasises the fact that although the records are kept on the same page, the Bank and Cash Accounts remain separate accounts.

Consider what happens when this £700 transfer is made. The money is taken out of the Cash Account − hence it appears on the credit side of Cash, because it is money leaving the account − and is entered on the debit side of the Bank Account, because it is money entering the Bank Account. Remember, the details written along-side the figures in ledger accounts merely indicate the name of the account where the second entry can be found. Thus, on the credit side of the Cash Account is written 'Bank' because it is the Bank Account that carries the second entry. Similarly, against the debit entry on the Bank Account can be seen the word 'Cash', showing that the opposite entry can be found in the Cash Account.

The recording of the transfer of money from the Cash Account to the Bank Account and vice versa gives rise to what are called **contra entries**. The word 'contra' simply means 'against', and it is usual to enter in the folio columns the letter 'C' to indicate that the double entry can be found on the opposite side of the same accounting record.

When at the end of the week the accounts are balanced, the debit entries are totalled − £990 and £2733 − as are the credit entries − £940 and £743 − and balances are struck for each of the accounts in the usual manner − £50 and £1990. These balances are then brought down to begin the next trading period.

Cash

			£				£
Oct 1	Balance		84	Oct 2	Purchases		180
	Sales		160		Windows		4
2	Sales		140	4	Wages		56
3	Sales		130	5	Bank		700
4	R Constable		36				940
	Sales		190		Balance		50
5	Sales		250				
			990				990
	Balance		50				

Cash Book

		Cash	Bank				Cash	Bank
		£	£				£	£
Oct 1	Balances	84	1 900	Oct 2	Purchases		180	
	Sales	160			Windows		4	
2	Sales	140		4	Wages		56	
3	J Taylor		76		R T Ltd			400
	G Williams		57		Em Co			320
	Sales	130		5	Petrol			23
4	R Constable	36			Bank	C	700	
	Sales	190					940	743
5	Sales	250			Balances		50	1 990
	Cash	C	700					
		990	2 733				990	2 733
6	Balances	50	1 990					

Bank

			£				£
Oct 1	Balance		1 900	Oct 4	R T Ltd		400
3	J Taylor		76		Em Co		320
	G Williams		57	5	Petrol		23
5	Cash		700				743
					Balance		1 990
			2 733				2 733
	Balance		1 990				

The accountant is concerned with safeguarding the company's monies and recording payments in and out of the business. The Sales Manager is also interested in those same figures and will be recording the sales information in his own way. From the above figures it is possible to obtain a good idea of the way the cash sales are going for October by preparing a bar chart as shown below.

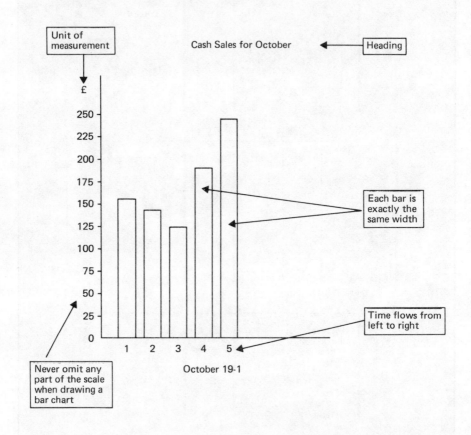

Overdrafts

In the example used, both the Cash Account and the Bank Account have debit balances on October 6. This indicates that the firm has an asset − cash − of £50 and an asset − money in the bank − of £1990. Remember, assets always have debit balances on these accounts.

However, it is possible for a business to draw more from its bank account than it has in it. This is called overdrawing and the amount that is overdrawn is known as an **overdraft**. It is usual to seek permission from the Bank Manager before overdrawing to ensure that the bank will honour the cheques. It is a criminal offence to issue cheques knowing that they will not be honoured by the bank.

An overdraft is a debt owed by a firm. As such, it is a liability, and like all liabilities, it reveals itself as a credit balance in the accounts.

If, in the example used, Em Co had been paid a cheque for £3320 by Numac on 4 October, the Cash Book would have appeared as on page 146. The firm would have spent £3743 from its Bank Account when it only possessed funds at the bank of £2733. The difference of £1010 (£3743 − £2733 = £1010) represents the size of the firm's overdraft at 6 October.

Although the Cash Book now shows a debit balance of £50 − indicating an asset (cash in the till) of £50 − the Cash Book also shows a credit balance in the Bank Account of £1010. This is an overdraft, and it is, of course, a liability. Remember, *a credit balance on a bank account in the Cash Book signifies an overdraft*.

Study carefully how the balance has been arrived at in this example.

Summary

On completion of this unit plus practice at the exercises, you should be able to:

1 Record business transactions in a two column Cash Book.

Cash Book

Debit (Receipts) side

Date	Particulars		£ (Cash)	£ (Bank)
Oct 1	Balances		84	1 900
2	Sales		160	
3	Sales		140	
	J Taylor			76
	G Williams			57
4	Sales		130	
	R Constable		36	
5	Sales		190	
	Sales		250	
	Cash	C		700
				2 733
				1 010
			990	3 743
			990	3 743
6	Balance		50	

Credit (Payments) side

Date	Particulars		£ (Cash)	£ (Bank)
Oct 2	Purchases		180	
4	Windows		4	
	Wages		56	
	R T Ltd			400
	Em Co			3 320
5	Petrol			23
	Bank	C	700	
	Balance		940	3 743
			50	
			990	3 743
6	*Balance*			1 010

Exercises

1   Draw up a two column Cash Book, and transfer to it the entries recorded in the following accounts:

Bank

		£				£
Sept 1	Capital	20 000	Sept 2	Cash		800
9	C Wilks	230		Premises	14	000
11	D Pavans	190		Fixtures	2	900
12	Sales	310		Purchases	1	400
16	Cash	300	10	Purchases		210
18	Rent rec'd	200	18	Drawings		180
24	Sales	132	22	S Williams		970
27	Cash	650	25	J Edwards		305
			29	C Eden		112
			30	Balance		
					c/d 1	135
		22 012			22	012
Oct 1	Balance	1 135				

Cash

		£			£
Sept 2	Bank	800	Sept 3	Stationery	27
3	Sales	104		Petrol	12
4	Sales	95	4	Advertising	14
6	D Owens	18	6	Wages	30
9	Sales	141	16	Bank	300
12	C Davis	37		Wages	30
14	Sales	317	21	Petrol	22
19	Sales	283	25	Wages	30
24	M Roberts	67	27	Bank	650
28	Sales	170	30	Balance	917
		2 032			2 032
Oct 1	Balance	917			

2   Explain the following terms in your own words:
current account   contra entry
deposit account   overdraft

Questions 3 − 7: enter the following transactions in a two column
Cash Book, and balance it at the end of the month.

3   June 1   Began business with £30 000 in the bank
          2   Transferred £500 from the bank to the Cash Account
          4   Paid by cheques for: premises £18 000, delivery van
              £2400, furniture and fittings £3700
          5   Paid for stocks by cheque £2840
          8   Cash sales £85
         10   Paid wages £46 and postage £8, both by cash
         14   Paid expenses by cheque: electricity £29, telephone
              £85, advertising £290
         15   Cash sales £374
         18   Received cheques from the following: R Thomas
              £98, D Lee £136, V Peach £220
         22   Cash sales £256, cash drawings £380
         24   Paid wages in cash £46
         28   Paid suppliers by cheque: L Pou £313, M Strudwick
              £402, D Storer £173
         29   Paid by cheque: rates £317, insurance £210
         30   Cash sales £332; S Wells paid his account cash £86

4   Feb   1   Balances: Cash in hand £190, Cash at bank £8010
          3   Paid insurance by cheque £530
          4   Paid for postage stamps, cash £17
          6   Cash sales £252
          7   Cash transferred from the till to the bank £204
          9   Paid E Wilson by cheque £225
         11   Paid A Hall in cash £7
         13   D Baker paid £510, £60 of it in cash, the remainder
              by cheque
         18   Cash drawings by the owner £68
         21   N Nutman paid by cheque £269
         24   £680 withdrawn from the bank for business use
         25   Paid cash for new furniture £663
         27   Paid rent by cheque £136
         28   Cash sales £357 paid direct into the bank

5 Apl 1 Began business with capital, cash £250
       2 Paid rent, cash £25
       3 Borrowed £1250 from P Morgan, received money by cheque
       4 Cash sales £245
       5 Paid R Wenham by cheque £162
       8 J Dix paid us by cheque £155
      10 Paid B Hart in cash £55
      13 Cash sales paid direct into bank £133
      15 J Rush paid us in cash £160
      17 Transferred £125 from Cash to Bank Account
      21 Repaid P Morgan by cheque £250
      24 Cash sales paid direct into the bank £165
      27 Paid motor expenses by cheque £30
      29 Withdrew £250 from bank for private use
      30 Paid for goods for resale by cheque £243

6 Aug 1 Balances: Cash £116 (Dr), Bank £2616 (Dr)
       4 Received cheque £480 from H Valance
       8 Paid the following by cheque: O Wend £230, P Savage £170
      12 Transferred £400 from bank to Cash Account
      17 Received cheques from J Bone £470, F Stand £310, E Butcher £340
      25 Paid salaries by cheque £5300
      26 Paid the following by cash: wages £168, petrol £50, postage £26, drawings £124
      27 Paid B Drain by cheque £228
      28 Received cash from T Baxter £70 and S Pound £90
      29 Paid A Wilt by cheque £416

7 May 1 Balances: Cash £258 (Dr), Bank £970 (Dr)
       2 Cash sales £74
       4 Paid rates by cheque £270
       5 Paid by cash for postage £14 and petrol £21
       6 Received cheque from T Winn £117
       8 Paid wages by cash £127
       9 Cash sales £215
      11 Paid the following by cheque: D Poidon £612, L Pound £252
      13 Received cash from B Jordan £38

22222222

2222

15 Cash sales £313; paid wages in cash £127
17 Paid insurance by cheque £320
19 Cash sales £281
23 Cash purchases £361
24 Drawings by cheque £238
25 Cash sales £262
27 Paid £500 from Cash to Bank Account
28 Received cheques from A Bates £300, B Brown £142, P Wills £111
29 Paid by cheque K Fawcett £214, T Bond £180, B Withers £604

11   Discounts

So far as the Bank and the Cash Accounts are concerned, the three column Cash Book operates in exactly the same way as the two column variety. The essential difference is that the three column Cash Book concerns itself with discounts. Before looking at the three column Cash Book, therefore, it is necessary to be clear on the differences between cash discount and trade discount.

A **discount** is a deduction from the price of goods, or from the amount due. Two forms of discount will be discussed: trade discount and cash discount.

Trade discount is a deduction given by a firm to customers in a similar line of business. Hence, a wholesaler may give trade discount to a retailer. Trade discount is never shown directly in the accounts; only the net amount is shown, after the discount has been deducted. Thus, when a firm buys goods on credit from Factum Ltd for £500 less 20% trade discount, the entries in the accounts will be to credit Factum Ltd with £400, and to debit the Purchases Account with £400. The £100 discount – i.e. 20% of £500 – will not be shown.

Cash discount is a deduction usually given for prompt payment. Cash discount is *always* shown in the accounts. It can be of two types:

discount allowed — cash discount allowed by the firm to its customers

discount received — cash discount received by the firm from its suppliers

Discount allowed is classed as an expense. It is recorded on the debit side of the Discount Allowed Account. Discount received is classed as a form of income, and it is recorded on the credit side of the Discount Received Account.

It is possible for trade and cash discounts to appear together. Thus, in the above example, Numac may have paid Factum Ltd promptly and been entitled to a further cash discount of 5%:

	£
Full purchase price	500
Less Trade discount of 20%	100
	400
Less Cash discount of 5%	20
Account paid	380

However, only the cash discount would appear in the accounts. Note too, that when the two forms of discount appear together, cash discount is calculated after trade discount has been deducted.

Three column Cash Books

The ruling for a three column Cash Book is shown opposite. It is the same as a two column Cash Book except that there is an additional column on each side of the Cash Book. On the debit side there is a column for discount allowed, and on the credit side, a column for discount received.

The following example shows how the three column Cash Book operates:

Nov 1   Balances: Cash £173 (Dr), Bank £2100 (Dr)
     2   Paid the following accounts, deducting 5% cash discount: D Appleby, cheque £260, E Scotter, cash £140
     3   The following customers paid their accounts, deducting $2^1/_2$% discount for prompt payment: G Kirton, cheque £120, H Brigg, cash £80
     4   Cash sales £190; paid postage, cash £14
     5   Bought goods £400 from N Scampton; paid by cheque after deducting 25% trade discount and 5% cash discount

The letters (Dr) after each of the opening balances indicate that they are debit balances. They are, therefore, entered on the debit side of the Cash Book.

Cash Book

Date	Particulars	Discount allowed £	Cash £	Bank £
Nov 1	Balances		173	2 100
3	G Kirton	3	78	
	H Brigg	2		117
4	Sales		190	
		5	441	2 217
6	Balances		294	1 685

Date	Particulars	Discount received £	Cash £	Bank £
Nov 2	D Appleby	13	133	247
2	E Scotter	7	14	
4	Postage			
5	Purchases			285
		20	147	532
	Balances		294	1 685
			441	2 217

On November 2 Numac paid two of its suppliers. The cash discount received is entered in the first column on the credit side of the Cash Book, and the net amount paid is entered in the bank and cash columns. The bank column thus shows the firm as having paid £247 to Appleby, and the cash column, £133 to Scotter. Remember, only the amount actually paid is entered in the bank and cash columns.

Similarly, on 3 November, when two of Numac's customers pay their debts, deducting $2^1/2\%$ cash discount, the amount of the discount is entered in the discount allowed column, and only the sum actually received goes into the cash and bank columns − £117 and £78.

On 5 November, the goods bought from Scampton are paid for at the time of purchase, so it is not necessary to provide an account for Scampton: he is neither a debtor nor a creditor. The goods are subject to 25% discount, but trade discount is not entered in the books at all, therefore only the net amount is entered: £400 − 25% = £300. However, from this £300, 5% cash discount must be deducted − and cash discounts are always shown in the books. Thus, the amount actually paid to Scampton is only £285, and this is the figure entered in the bank column. Note that the £15 is not entered in the discount column in this instance because the items have been paid for.

At the end of the week, the Cash Book is balanced in the usual manner. The total of the discounts allowed is transferred to the Discount Allowed Account, while the total of the discounts received is transferred to the Discount Received Account. They would each appear as below. Note that discount allowed, being an expense,

Discount Allowed

	£
Nov 6 Total for week	5

Discount Received

	£
Nov 6 Total for week	20

shows as a debit balance, while discount received, being a form of income, appears as a credit balance.

To complete the exercise, it is necessary to look at the accounts of the debtors and creditors. In each case, it is assumed that the total amount outstanding has been paid.

D Appleby

	£		£
Nov 2 Bank	247	Nov 1 Balance	260
Disc. rec'd	13		
	260		260

E Scotter

	£		£
Nov 2 Cash	133	Nov 1 Balance	140
Disc. rec'd	7		
	140		140

G Kirton

	£		£
Nov 1 Balance	120	Nov 3 Bank	117
		Disc. all'd	3
	120		120

H Brigg

	£		£
Nov 1 Balance	80	Nov 3 Cash	78
		Disc. all'd	2
	80		80

On Appleby's Account, although Numac has paid only £247, the whole debt of £260 is considered to have been settled: the £13 is the discount received. This £13 is therefore entered on the debit side of the account, along with the record of the payment. The double entry for the £13 appears as part of the discount received figure of £20 (£13 + £7 = £20) on the credit side of the Discount Received Account. The double entry for the £247 appears on the credit side of the Bank Account.

Note, therefore, that the discount column in the Cash Book is *not* part of the double entry. It is merely a memorandum: an aid to the accounting record, The double entry for the discount received is to debit the supplier's account, and to credit the Discount Received Account.

When H Brigg pays £78 in cash, his account is credited and the Cash Account debited. The £2 discount allowed forms part of the £5 weekly total on the credit side of the Discount Allowed Account (£2 + £3 = £5). The double entry for this is on the credit side of Brigg's Account. Again, the discount column in the Cash Book is simply a memorandum: it is not part of the double entry.

The above example illustrates that cash discount is available whether payment is made by cash or by cheque: it is not restricted merely to cash transactions.

Trial Balance

In the Trial Balance, the Discount Allowed Account will appear in the list of debit balances, whilst the Discount Received Account will appear in the list of credit balances.

Extract of Trial Balance		
	£	£
Discounts	310	580

In the above example, therefore, £310 is the balance on the Discount Allowed Account and £580 is the balance on the Discount Received Account.

Profit & Loss Account

Discount allowed is an expense. As such it is transferred to the debit side of the Profit and Loss Account at the end of the accounting period, along with all the other expenses. In contrast, discount received is a form of income, so the balance on the Discount Received Account is transferred to the credit side of Profit and Loss Account at the end of the period.

```
                    Discount  Allowed
                         £                              £
    Balance             310   Profit & Loss            310

                 Profit & Loss  Account
                         £                              £
    Wages                xx   Gross profit             xx
    Rent & rates         xx   Discount received       580
    Discount allowed    310

                    Discount  Received
                         £                              £
    Profit & Loss       580   Balance                 580
```

Using the earlier figures, the balance of £310 on the debit side of Discount Allowed Account is transferred to the debit side of Profit and Loss Account. The credit balance of £580 on the Discount Received Account is, in its turn, transferred to the credit side of the Profit and Loss Account.

Note that in both cases the discount accounts are closed after this transfer operation.

Summary

On completion of this unit plus practice at the exercises you should be able to:

1 State the difference between cash and trade discount, and explain how each is handled in the accounts.
2 Prepare a three column Cash Book from information supplied.
3 Recognise discounts allowed and discounts received in a Trial Balance.
4 Prepare a Profit and Loss Account which includes discounts allowed and discounts received.

Exercises

1 Explain the meaning of each entry in the following accounts:

```
                          N Evans
                          £                              £
Jan  1 Balance           280   Jan 10 Bank             266
    14 Sales             150           Disc. all'd      14
    21 Sales              70        31 Balance          220
                         ───                            ───
                         500                            500
                         ═══                            ═══
Feb  1 Balance           220

                        T Greenwood
                          £                              £
Mar  8 Bank              504   Mar  1 Balance          560
       Disc. all'd        56        17 Purchases       140
    31 Balance           140
                         ───                            ───
                         700                            700
                         ═══                            ═══
                               Apr  1 Balance          140
```

2   What is the difference between cash discount and trade discount?

3   From the following information show the account of J Podger in the books of Numac Trading Co.

Nov 1   Balance £280 (Cr)
     18   Numac purchased items on credit from Podger £400 less 20% trade discount
     24   Numac purchased further items for £120 less 33$^1/_3$% trade discount
     30   Numac paid off the debt to Podger by cheque, deducting 10% cash discount

4   Use the following information to prepare the account of N Flogg in Numac's books

Oct 1   Balance £190 (Dr)
     12   Sold to Flogg items on credit £360 less 25% trade discount
     26   Sold further items to Flogg on credit £300 less 20% trade discount
     30   Flogg paid off his account in full by cheque, deducting 5% cash discount

Questions 5 and 6: enter the transactions in the three column Cash Book, balance the book at the end of the month and show the discount accounts as they would appear at the month end.

5   May 1   Balances: Cash £405 (Dr), Bank £5600 (Dr)
          5   Cash sales £335
          6   Purchases paid for by cheque £1580
          7   Paid cheques to A D Garages £67 and for rates £249
          8   Received cheques from the following who each deducted 2$^1/_2$% cash discount from the sums shown: B Downs £200, H Gait £120, D Heath £240
          9   Paid for postage, cash £8
         11   Paid the following debts by cheque, deducting a cash discount of 5% in each case: T Gunter £360, B Cowie £280, J Turner £140
         13   Cash sales £346
         14   Drawings by cheque £383
         16   Paid wages in cash £290

17 Cash sales £271

19 Paid electricity by cheque £49

23 The following customers paid their accounts deducting a cash discount of 2¹/₂%: F Reynolds £160, R Waite £280, B Coleman £80

25 Transferred £600 from Cash to Bank Account

27 Paid the following suppliers by cheque deducting a cash discount of 5%: D Pope £400, S Hobbs £340, P Lamb £240

29 Paid salaries by cheque £3720

6 July 1 Balances: Cash £570 (Dr), Bank £6420 (Dr)

3 Paid by cheque insurance £174, rent £98, heating £386

4 Cash sales £194

7 Cash sales £256

9 Paid wages in cash £417

10 Received cheques from the following, who each deducted a cash discount of 5%: S Drake £100, B Fowles £140, K Kenneth £160

14 Paid by cheque the following, deducting 7¹/₂% cash discount: H Bowler £200, P Turpin £320, V Rakes £360

16 Cash sales £312; paid in cash: wages £417, window cleaner £5; purchases £56

18 Cash sales £294

23 Paid cash for advertising £17, wages £417

24 Drawings £380, £80 in cash, the remainder by cheque

25 The following customers paid by cheque, deducting a cash discount of 5%: B Leu £250, S Small £200, W Bond £120

27 Paid by cheque, deducting a cash discount of 7¹/₂%: C Vowles £160, A Lucas £280, H Philips £120

Questions 7, 8, 9: you are asked to produce Profit and Loss Accounts for the year ended as at the Trial Balance date, and the discount accounts as at that date.

7   KNOWLE TRADING CO

Extract of Trial Balance as at 31 December 19-4

	£	£
Discounts	410	620
Wages	12 480	
Rent and rates	3 260	
General expenses	1 460	
Gross profit		25 500

8   CLIFTON RETAILING

Extract of Trial Balance as at 31 March 19-6

	£	£
Gross profit		26 410
Discounts	810	1 130
Lighting and heating	1 680	
Wages and salaries	13 950	
Miscellaneous expenses	1 860	
Rent received		1 460

9   HARTCLIFFE GROCERIES

Extract of Trial Balance as at 30 September 19-6

	£	£
Administration expenses	2 310	
Salaries	16 420	
Advertising	1 260	
Sundry expenses	1 340	
Discounts	770	1 140
Interest received		260
Gross profit		18 070

12 Bank reconciliation statements

A business will keep a record of its bank transactions in its Cash Book, debiting those amounts which are paid into the account, and crediting those sums which are withdrawn. The sums paid into the bank will be accompanied by a **paying-in slip**. This shows details of what was paid in, when, and by whom. It also shows the account number. The counterfoil carries similar information, and will be retained by the account holder for his own records. (See Fig. 7)

In most cases, a firm's bank account is a **current account**. Money in a current account can be withdrawn at will, and for this purpose the bank will provide the business with a cheque book. A **cheque** is a written instruction to the bank to pay money to the person named on the cheque.

Two forms of cheque are used. An open cheque, shown in Fig. 8, can be exchanged over the bank counter for money without any record being kept as to who is receiving the money. A crossed cheque, on the other hand, can only be paid into a bank account. (See Fig. 9). This enables some record to be kept as to who has cashed the cheque. In general, firms use crossed cheques because they minimise the risk of cheques being stolen; if a thief tries to cash a crossed cheque, he must do so through a bank account, and he will thus be traceable.

Although money in a current account is available on demand, it does not carry interest. The other form of bank account, the **deposit account**, does earn interest, but banks can demand advance notice of any withdrawals. In addition, it is not usually possible to overdraw on a deposit account. Deposit accounts, generally, are used for money which is likely to be banked for lengthy periods.

With all the activity which is normal on a current account, it is important that the firm and the bank agree over the amount of money which the firm has in the account. For this reason, the bank will periodically submit a **bank statement** to the business.

Figure 7

Left slip:

DATE 23rd February 1979
CREDIT THE ACCOUNT OF C Brown

	£	
£20 notes . .		
£10 notes . .		
£5 notes . .		
£1 notes . .	20	00
50p	12	50
Silver		50
Bronze . . .		
TOTAL CASH	33	00
Postal Orders .		
Cheques, etc.	267	00
TOTAL CREDIT £	300	00

Right slip:

SPECIMEN ONLY Issued by Bank Education Service.

DATE 23rd February 1979
Bank of Education
CREDIT

	£	
£20 notes . .		
£10 notes . .		
£5 notes . .		
£1 notes . . .	20	00
50p . . .	12	50
Silver		50
Bronze . . .		
TOTAL CASH	33	00
Postal Orders .		
Cheques, etc. (Listed overleaf)	267	00

ACCOUNT C BROWN
ACCOUNT NUMBER 10476375 £ 300 00

Paid in by C Brown

Customers are advised that the Bank reserves the right at its discretion to postpone payment of cheques drawn against uncleared effects which may have been credited to the account

Figure 8

SPECIMEN ONLY Issued by Bank Education Service.

21st May 1979

21st May 1979 00-00-00

BANK OF EDUCATION
HOMETOWN

Mrs Elsie Brown

Pay Mrs Elsie Brown _____ or Order

Twenty five pounds only £25—00

£25—00

000651 ⑈000651⑈ 00⑈0000: 10476375⑈ 30

Figure 9

SPECIMEN ONLY Issued by Bank Education Service.

29th May 1979

29th May 1979 00-00-00

BANK OF EDUCATION
HOMETOWN

J H Brown

Pay J H Brown _____ or Order

Twenty five pounds only £25—00

£25—00

000651 ⑈000651⑈ 00⑈0000: 10476375⑈ 30

The bank statement

The bank statement shows the opening balance on the account along with all the amounts paid in and withdrawn during the period. It also shows the amount which the firm still has in the account.

Nowadays, the statement is prepared by a computerised system. The presentation of the information differs from the double entry presentation used earlier. However, the double entry *principles,* still apply: it is only the *presentation* of the account which differs.

The statement carries the name and address of the account holder and the account number. It shows the receipts and payments as they have accrued and, after each transaction, the balance on the account is amended. This balance is shown in the right-hand column.

This three-column presentation of accounts, with a running total for the balance is quite common wherever mechanised or computerised accounting systems are used. Indeed, the term 'current account' comes from the French word 'courant' meaning 'running': the account provides a running total from day to day.

The bank statement conforms to orthodox double entry principles. So long as the account holder has money in his account, he is a creditor of the bank: the bank owes him money. Thus, in the bank's records, his account will show a credit balance. In his own records, money in the bank is an asset, and it thus appears as a debit balance.

However, should the customer overdraw, he becomes a debtor of the bank: he owes the bank money. In the bank's records, his account will show a debit balance, while in his own records, since the bank is now one of his creditors, the overdraft will appear as a credit balance.

On many bank statements, overdrafts are thus printed with the letters DR after the amount. Sometimes O/D may appear: this means overdrawn. In earlier times, overdrafts appeared on a bank statement in red ink, hence the term 'going into the red'. This practice has now largely died out.

Reconciliation statements

Although the bank statement provides a check on the Cash Book, there are a number of reasons why the balance as shown on the Cash Book will not exactly equal that shown on the statement.

It may be that a mistake has been made, either by the business or by the bank. Alternatively, someone may have been falsifying the records deliberately to hide pilfering from the till. More usually, however, the differences will arise because of the time delay between entries being made in the Cash Book, and entries being made by the bank.

When Numac writes out a cheque to pay one of its suppliers, the entry is made on the credit side of the Cash Book almost immediately. The cheque, however, has to be sent to the supplier, and he has to take it to his bank where it goes through the bank's processes before Numac's bank is presented with it.

This process can take three or four days. If, during that period, Numac's bank prepares a statement for the firm, this cheque will not appear on the statement because the bank is ignorant of its existence. In order for the bank statement figure to agree with the Cash Book figure, the amount of this cheque must either be added back to the Cash Book total, or deducted from the bank statement figure.

Assume that the cheque in question was paid to Universal Supplies on Monday 1 October, and that the Cash Book was credited with £75 on that day. If the account is now balanced, the Cash Book will show £1175 in the Bank Account. However, the cheque does not reach Universal Supplies until Wednesday, they bank it on Thursday and it does not arrive at Numac's bank until Friday.

```
                    NUMAC TRADING CO
                 Extract from Cash Book
                        £                                £
   Oct 1 Balance      1 250      Oct 1 Universal
                                       Supplies          75
                                       Balance        1 175

                     _____                          _____
                      1 250                            1 250
                     ======                          ======
   Oct 2 Balance      1 175
```

If the bank had sent Numac a bank statement on Tuesday, it would show the firm as having £1250 in its account. To see whether the difference between the Cash Book's £1175 and the statement's £1250 can be accounted for, some reconciliation has to be made. In other words, the difference must be explained. This explanation appears in the form of a **reconciliation statement**.

Bank reconciliation statements			
a	£	*b*	£
from bank statement		*from Cash Book*	
Balance at bank as bank statement	1 250	Cash Book balance	1 175
Less Cheques drawn but not presented	75	*Add* Cheque drawn but not presented	75
Cash Book balance	1 175	Balance as per bank statement	1 250

It makes no difference whether the reconciliation begins with the Cash Book balance and works towards the bank statement, or vice versa. Each approach is acceptable. What does matter is that one remembers from which record the exercise is begun. Notice that the £75 is deducted from the bank statement figure in *a* because the cheque does not appear on the statement: the statement thus over-states the true position.

However, the £75 is added to the Cash Book balance in *b* because the cheque has yet to reach the bank; the £75 must be added back to the Cash Book to make the two records comparable.

Consider a more complicated example. Numac's bank statement for the first weeks in November, and the firm's Cash Book for the same period are shown opposite.

By studying the two documents, one can readily see that the balance at the bank, as recorded by the firm's Cash Book, is £280, whereas the bank statement shows a balance of £300.

Further investigation shows that cheques have been sent to Factors Ltd £86 and to Lewis Jones £74, but that these have not yet been presented for payment: they are still in the post. The cheques payable to the Electricity Board £75 and Demat Co £47 do appear on the bank statement, showing that these have been presented.

```
                    NUMAC TRADING CO
                    Bank statement

  Date   Particulars        Payments   Receipts   Balance
  19-1                          £          £          £
  Nov 1 Balance forward                            292 00
      2 Cash                            120 00     412 00
      8 Cheque no  712       75 00                 337 00
      9 Cheque no  713       47 00                 290 00
     10 Charges              10 00                 280 00
        Bank int                         20 00     300 00
```

```
                    NUMAC TRADING CO
         Extract from Cash Book (Bank columns only)

                        £                            £
  Nov 1 Balance        292    Nov 5 Electricity     75
      2 Cash           120          Demat Co        47
     10 Green           98        9 Factors Ltd     86
        Brown           52          Lewis, Jones    74
                                 10 Balance        280
                       ___                         ___
                       562                         562
                       ===                         ===
     11 Balance        280
```

The firm has received cheques on 10 November from Green £98, and Brown £52. Although these have been entered in the Cash Book, they have not yet been banked, since no record of them appears on the bank statement.

The bank has charged the firm £10 for bank charges, and has entered £20 bank interest received in the current account, but no record of either of these appears in the Cash Book.

The task now is to explain the differing balances of £280 and £300 by means of the bank reconciliation statement. As stated above, it does not matter whether one begins with the £280 and works back to the £300 or vice versa.

If the reconciliation begins with the Cash Book balance, the calculation proceeds as shown below. The cheques to Factors and to Lewis, Jones which have been deducted from the Cash Book are added back, because they have not been deducted from the bank's figure. Bank interest has been included in the bank statement figure, but not in the Cash Book, so it must be added to the Cash Book balance.

The cheques received but not banked have been included in the Cash Book balance, but not in the bank statement balance, so these are deducted. Bank charges have been deducted in arriving at the bank statement figure, but they have not been subtracted from the Cash Book balance, so these, too, are deducted.

```
                NUMAC TRADING CO

           Bank reconciliation statement
                11 November 19-1

                                           £        £
Cash Book balance                                  280
Add Cheques drawn but not presented
        Factors Ltd                        86
        Lewis, Jones                       74
                                          ──
                                                   160
                                                  ────
                                                   440
Add Bank interest                                   20
                                                  ────
                                                   460

Less Cheques received but not presented
        Green                              98
        Brown                              52
                                          ──
                                                   150
                                                  ────
                                                   310
Less Bank charges                                   10
                                                  ────
Bank statement balance                             300
                                                  ════
```

In this way, the Cash Book balance of £280 is reconciled with the bank statement balance of £300. In other words, the difference between the two figures can be explained. If the difference cannot be explained, then further investigation must be made, mistakes looked for or fraud suspected.

If the reconciliation had begun with the balance on the bank statement, the calculation would appear as shown below. Cheques received but not banked have been included in the Cash Book record, but they do not yet appear in the bank's record, so they must be added on. Similarly with bank charges: they have been deducted in the bank's records but not in the Cash Book, so to make the balances comparable, the £10 must be added back to the bank figure.

```
                    NUMAC TRADING CO

              Bank reconciliation statement
                   11 November 19-1

                                            £        £
Bank statement balance                               300
Add Cheques received but not presented
        Green                               98
        Brown                               52
                                            ──
                                                     150
                                                     ──
                                                     450
        Bank charges                                  10
                                                     ──
                                                     460
Less Cheques drawn but not presented
        Factors Ltd                         86
        Lewis, Jones                        74
                                            ──
                                                     160
                                                     ──
                                                     300
        Bank interest                                 20
                                                     ──
Cash Book balance                                    280
                                                     ══
```

The cheques to Factors and to Lewis, Jones have been deducted in the calculation of the Cash Book balance, so they must be deducted from the bank's figures to make the bank statement balance comparable. The bank interest has been included in the bank statement, but not in the Cash Book so it, too, must be deducted.

In this way, by making the bank's figures comparable with the Cash Book balance, the differences can be explained, and errors highlighted.

This reconciliation process will occur every time the firm receives its bank statement. Not only will the figures within the statement be checked, but the closing balance as recorded by the bank will be verified in this way.

Summary

On completion of this unit plus practice at the exercises you should be able to:

1 Reconcile the bank balance in the Cash Book with that shown on the bank statement.
2 Explain how the differences have occurred.
3 Be able to use the necessary documents.

Exercises

1 Explain the meaning of:
crossed cheque   overdraft
current account   paying-in slip
deposit account   standing order
direct debit

2 Why do firms usually use a current account for their business bank account?

3 For what reasons may differences arise between the Cash Book bank balance, and that shown on a bank statement?

4 The balance shown on B Charlton's bank statement was £773 credit, yet the firm's Cash Book showed only £763 in the bank.

Further inspection showed that whilst the following cheques had been received and recorded in the Cash Book, they had not yet been banked: Arnetta Trading Co £196, V Grey £48, L Malet £219.

The following cheques had been sent to suppliers, but had yet to be presented for payment: P Davison Associates £312, Higatt Industries Ltd £115, Hayes, Hoyland Ltd £78. Bank charges of £32 appeared in the statement but not in the Cash Book.

Produce a bank reconciliation statement to explain the differences in the two bank figures

a starting with the bank statement balance and
b starting with the Cash Book balance.

5   The Cash Book of St Martin Trading Co showed the firm as having £753 in the bank, but the bank statement showed £1547 credit. Bank charges of £23 did not appear in the Cash Book, neither did bank interest of £219 paid into the current account.

The following cheques were recorded in the Cash Book as received, but they had not been banked: M Rice £79, C Holmes £145, P Jenkins £204. Cheques paid, but not presented to the bank for payment were Benjamin Hope Ltd £364, T Martin & Co £239, O Brian & Co Ltd £423.

Produce a bank reconciliation statement to explain the differences in the two bank figures

a starting with the bank statement balance and
b starting with the Cash Book balance.

6   According to A Bredski's bank statement, her business had an overdraft of £836. She is concerned since her own records show an overdraft of only £281. However, she has yet to bank the following cheques received from her customers: D Crawford £128, B May £64, R Kemp £227, J Allan £735.

The following standing orders were paid by the bank, but they had not been recorded in the Cash Book: National Retailers Association £36, Chamber of Commerce £29. The following cheques had been sent to suppliers, but had not yet been presented for payment: Mercia Electricity Board £83, Hallomshire County Council £476, W Jackson & Son Ltd £105.

Show A Bredski how the differences between her own records and those of the bank may have arisen.

7   Stan Nicholls has received a letter from his bank manager pointing out that his business bank account is £426 overdrawn. His own Cash Book shows an overdraft of £119. The following cheques sent to suppliers have not been presented for payment: Garer Manufacturing Co £217, Wills, Reid & Co £145, L Lock Ltd £174, Miller & Co £86.

Standing orders not recorded in the Cash Book are £378 to the Commercial Building Society and £24 to the Association of Retail Management. Customers' cheques still waiting to be banked are S Graham £52, A McTavish £143, R Hardy £96, Drinkwater & Sons £236.

Show Stan how the differences in the two bank balances can be reconciled.

13 Subsidiary books

Unit 11 explained how memorandum columns were used in the three column Cash Book to collect information concerning cash discounts received and cash discounts allowed. These memorandum columns were not part of the double entry, but were used to help record business activity.

The idea of keeping records to help in the writing up of the ledger is extended even further to subsidiary books of account. Like the discount columns in the Cash Book, these books are merely supplementary to the double entry system; they are not part of it. The four books which will be examined are:

Sales Journal
Purchases Journal
Purchases Returns Book
Sales Returns Book

The subsidiary books themselves are written up from **prime documents**. As the name suggests, prime documents are those items which start off the whole accounting sequence. Documents such as copy invoices, orders received, debit and credit notes fall into this category. Students who are unfamiliar with such prime documents should refer to Appendix A which describes their individual purposes more fully.

Sales Journal

The Sales Journal — sometimes called the Sales Day Book — records only credit sales. Cash sales, or sales made in return for cheques are recorded in the Cash Book.

The Sales Journal is merely a list of credit sales in a given period — a day, week or month. At the end of the period the journal is totalled, and the grand figure of credit sales for that month is transferred to the Sales Account.

Assume that Numac's credit sales for the week are:

Sept 14   Goods to D Edford £28
    15   Goods to S Wells £46
    16   Items to B Gurney £37
    17   Items to D Edford £29

Using the system developed so far, the entries would be:

```
                             Sales
                                                        £
                              Sept 14 D Edford         28
                                   15 S Wells          46
                                   16 B Gurney         37
                                   17 D Edford         29

                    D Edford
                    £
Sept 14 Sales       28
     17 Sales       29

                    S Wells
                    £
Sept 15 Sales       46

                    B Gurney
                    £
Sept 16 Sales       37
```

However, if a Sales Journal were used, the credit sales would be listed in it as on page 175, and the *total* transferred to the Sales Account.

The Sales Account would carry the total figure of £140, and not the individual entries. The double entry rule would still be obeyed since the debit entries would appear on the customers' accounts; these remain unchanged. The credit entry now becomes a composite or total figure on the Sales Account.

Not only does the journal avoid cluttering the Sales Account with numerous small entries, but it also allows the job of recording business transactions to be split among different people. It may be

```
                         Sales Journal
                                   Invoice No          £
Sept 14  D Edford                  1273                28
     15  S Wells                   1274                46
     16  B Gurney                  1275                37
     17  D Edford                  1276                29
                                                      ───
         Total for the week,                          140
         transferred to Sales Account                 ═══
```

```
                            Sales
                                                       £
                            Sept 17 Total credit
                                    sales for
                                    week             140
```

that the Sales Journal can be kept at the point of sale − e.g. in the kiosk at a garage − while the customers' accounts are kept in the firm's main office. The forecourt attendant can complete the Sales Journal, while the accounting staff can take charge of the ledger entries.

In some firms the Sales Journal is written up from copies of the invoices which have been sent to the customers. Where this is so, the invoice number may well be entered in the Sales Journal against the customer's name.

Purchases Journal

The Purchases Journal − sometimes called the Purchases Day Book − is used to record credit purchases, but not, of course, the purchase of fixed assets. As was seen earlier, the purchase of fixed assets needs special attention. Purchases made for cheque or cash will appear in the Cash Book.

The Purchases Journal works in a similar way to the Sales Journal. Credit purchases for the period are listed, and at the end of the period the total is transferred to the Purchases Account. The creditors' accounts remain as normal.

The Purchases Journal is used as follows to record the following credit purchases of Numac Co for one week:

Sept 21 Goods bought from C Frome £140
    23 Items from W Mells Ltd £70
    25 Goods from G Elm £80
    26 Goods from W Mells Ltd £110

```
                    Purchases Journal
                                    Order No              £
Sept 21   C Frome                   2361                140
     23   W Mells Ltd               2362                 70
     25   G Elm                     2363                 80
     26   W Mells Ltd               2364                110

          Total for month,                              ___
          transferred to Purchases Account             400
                                                       ===

                         Purchases
                            £
Sept 30 Total credit
        purchases
        for month     400

                          C Frome
                                                          £
                                  Sept 21 Purchases      140

                        W Mells Ltd
                                                          £
                                  Sept 23 Purchases       70
                                       26 Purchases      110

                           G Elm
                                                          £
                                  Sept 25 Purchases       80
```

Once again, the basic double entry rules have been kept. The credit entries appear on the creditors' accounts, while the debit entry appears as a composite figure on the Purchases Account.

The Purchases Journal will be written up from copies of the firm's orders. Where this is done, the relevant order number may well appear alongside the supplier's name in the Purchases Journal.

Purchases returns

The Purchases Returns Book – or the Returns Outwards Book – records those items of stock which have been returned by the firm to its suppliers. It records *all* such returns, whether purchased on credit, for cash, or by cheque.

Items might be returned because they were not of the type, colour or size originally ordered. They might also be returned because they were received in a damaged condition, were of short weight, or were in some other way unsaleable. At the end of the period, the total of the Purchases Returns Book is transferred to the credit side of the Returns Outwards Account.

The following items were returned by Numac Trading Co to its suppliers during October:

Oct 2 Goods previously bought on credit from D Dorset £200, £20 now returned
   18 Returned goods bought by cash from F Kent £14
   26 Returned items bought by cheque from B Avon £16.

The Purchases Returns Book would appear as follows:

Purchases Returns Book		
	Debit note	£
Oct 2 D Dorset	132	20
18 F Kent	133	14
26 B Avon	134	16
Total for month transferred to Returns Outwards Account		50

The Returns Outwards Account would show the total returns:

Returns Outward		
		£
	Oct 30 Total for month	50

Debit notes would be issued, and the suppliers' accounts would appear as follows:

D Dorset				
	£			£
Oct 2 Returns out.	20	Oct 1 Balance		200
Balance	*180*			
	200			200
		3 *Balance*		*180*

F Kent	
	£
Oct 18 Returns out.	14

B Avon	
	£
Oct 26 Returns out.	16

In each case, the entry appears on the debit side of the supplier's account. The firm's debt to Dorset is reduced by £20 through the return of the goods.

With Kent and Avon, these suppliers were paid at the time of purchase. It is necessary, therefore, to create accounts for each of them to record the fact that goods have been paid for which have since been returned. Note that both Kent and Avon end up with debit balances, indicating that they are, in fact, debtors to the firm: they owe Numac Trading Co for the returned goods.

Where debit notes are used, the Purchases Returns Book is written up from copies of them, with the relevant numbers entered in the Book.

In Dorset's case, Numac returns goods valued at £20. The effect of this is to reduce Numac's debt to Dorset. This reduction in Numac's debt is recorded by entering the £20 on the debit side of Dorset's Account. In other words, Dorset's Account has been debited with £20. This is how 'debit note' got its name.

Sales returns

The Sales Returns Book — or Returns Inwards Book — records those items which are returned to the firm by its customers. It records all such returns, whether the goods were sold on credit or not. The reasons for customers returning items are as varied as the reasons for the firm sending items back to its suppliers. In some cases, goods returned by customers will in turn be sent on by the firm to its suppliers, since the reason for the items' return may be due to a manufacturer's fault.

At the end of the period, the total of the Sales Returns Book is transferred to the debit side of the Returns Inwards Account.

The following items were returned to Numac during November:

Nov   7   A Down had bought goods on credit on Nov 5 for £56; he returned £6 of goods because they were faulty

      16   B Side returned items he had bought for cash £4

      29   C Long returned items he had purchased by cheque £20

The Sales Returns Book and the Returns Inwards Account would appear as follows:

Sales Returns Book		
	Credit note	£
Nov 7 A Down	222	6
16 B Side	223	4
29 C Long	224	20
Total for month transferred to Returns Inwards Account		30

Returns Inwards		
	£	
Nov 30 Total for month	30	

A Down				
	£			£
Nov 5 Sales	56	Nov 7 Returns in		6
		Balance		*50*
	56			56
8 *Balance*	*50*			

B Side		
		£
	Nov 16 Returns in	4

C.Long		
		£
	Nov 29 Returns in	20

A Down's debt of £56 is reduced by his return of the goods. Side and Long had already paid for their items before they had cause to return them. They, therefore, become creditors of the firm until such time as the goods are replaced, or they purchase further items. Separate accounts are raised for each of them, showing credit balances.

The Sales Returns Book may well be written up from the copies of credit notes which the firm issues to those customers who have returned goods.

In Down's case, he will be issued with a credit note for £6, since he has returned £6 worth of goods. In doing this, he has reduced his indebtedness to the firm. This reduction in his debt is recorded by making an entry on the credit side of his account. In other words, he has been credited with £6. Hence the name given to the credit note.

Trial Balance

As will be seen from the above examples, the Returns Inwards Account will always show a debit balance, while the Returns Outwards Account will always show a credit balance. Thus, if both Returns Accounts are given on the same line in the Trial Balance, it is relatively simple to discover which is which.

Extract from Trial Balance		
	£	£
Returns inwards and outwards	260	500

In the Trial Balance extract above, the £260 appears in the list of debit balances: it must clearly be the balance on the Returns Inwards Account. The £500 which appears in the list of credit balances must be the balance on the Returns Outwards Account.

Trading Account

When the Trading Account is prepared, the total of the Returns Inwards Account is transferred to it, and this figure is usually deducted from the sales figure. Similarly, the Returns Outwards total is deducted from the purchases figure.

If Numac's returns inwards for the quarter amounted to £260, and the returns outwards to £500, then the Trading Account would appear as on page 182.

By subtracting the returns figures from purchases and sales the double entry rules have been broken, but this is done to give an indication of net purchases and net sales just as earlier, the closing stock was subtracted to find the cost of goods sold. If the Trading Account is redrafted according to strict double entry rules, the figure for gross profit will still be £3800.

The Trading Account is usually prepared from a Trial Balance. Where this is so, it is important to subtract the correct returns figure from purchases and from sales. This is quite simple if one remem-

NUMAC TRADING CO

Trading Account for the three months ended 31 December 19-6

		£			£
Opening stock		4 000	Sales		15 460
Add			Less Returns in		260
Purchases	12 400				
Less					
Returns out	500				
		11 900			
		15 900			
Less Closing stock		4 500			
Cost of goods sold		11 400			
Gross profit		3 800			
		15 200			15 200

Returns Inwards

	£		£
Dec 31 Balance	260	Dec 31 Trading	260

Returns Outwards

	£		£
Dec 31 Trading	500	Dec 31 Balance	500

bers the cross of St Andrew. The figure to be deducted from sales is the one that appears in the list of *debit* balances, while the figure to be deducted from purchases is the one which appears in the list of *credit* balances.

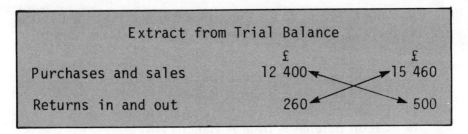

In the above example, the £260 is deducted from the sales figure of £15 460, and the £500 is deducted from the purchases figure of £12 400.

Summary

On completion of this unit plus practice at the exercises you should be able to:

1 Explain the purpose of subsidiary books in the accounting system.
2 Produce from information supplied a Sales Journal, Purchases Journal, Sales Returns Book and Purchases Returns Book.
3 Recognise purchases and sales returns in a Trial Balance.
4 Adjust the Trading Account to accommodate purchases and sales returns.

Exercises

1 Write up the Sales Journal from the following. Post the items to the relevant debtors' accounts and show the transfer to the Sales Account:

Jan 1 Credit sales to J Curtis £273
5 Credit sales to T Young £186
9 Credit sales to M Printing £77
16 Credit sales to T Young £214
23 Credit sales to M Printing £123
29 Credit sales to J Curtis £317

2   Enter the following in the Purchases Journal. Post the items to the creditors' accounts and show the transfer to the Purchases Account.

Feb 2   Credit purchases from J Harrison £497
      7   Credit purchases from A Hill £364
     14   Credit purchases from P Hutchinson £149
     19   Credit purchases from A Baker £518
     24   Credit purchases from C Tomkins £83
     26   Credit purchases from A Hill £236
     28   Credit purchases from J Harrison £223

Questions 3 and 4: write up the Sales, Purchases, Returns In and Returns Out Journal from the following information. Enter the transactions in the debtors' and the creditors' accounts, and transfer the totals of the journals to the Sales, Purchases and Returns Accounts.

3   Mar 1   Credit purchases from J Scott £217, T Whitfield £391, B Cooke £422
         3   Credit sales to P Smart £73, J Gardiner £48, P Ryan £36
         5   Credit purchases: B Cooke £84, K Fortune £114, G Collins £79
        12   Goods returned to us by P Smart £13, P Ryan £4
        16   Credit sales to P Smart £46, S Haze £27, T Boyd £35
        19   We returned goods to J Scott £27, B Cooke £12, G Collins £8
        25   Credit sales to R Camel £19, K Steele £32, J Amos £15
        28   Credit purchases: T Whitfield £94, B Cooke £76, B Todd £91
        30   We returned goods to B Todd £6, B Cooke £9, K Fortune £14

4   April 2   Credit sales to: M Gordon £18, D Parfitt £47, S Briant £57
           5   Credit purchases: S Ratcliff £117, M Copsey £263, A Morris £312
           7   Goods returned to us by M Gordon £2, S Briant £7
           9   Credit purchases: J Freeman £372, G Toll £223, A Morris £183
          14   Goods returned by us to: M Copsey £23, A Morris £32, G Tall £17

16 Credit sales B Hepton £72, D Parfitt £43, R Pember £54
18 Credit purchases: J Freeman £114, G Tall £96, R Rose £241
22 Goods returned by us to R Rose £18, G Tall £4
27 Credit sales B Hepton £27, S Briant £49, A Richards £69
29 Goods returned to us by B Hepton £12, R Pember £9

5 Explain carefully the significance of each of the entries in the following accounts.

D Broome

	£		£
Sept 4 Bank	432	Sept 1 Balance	480
Disc. rec'd	48	9 Purchases	138
16 Returns out	37	28 Purchases	262
30 Balance	363		
	880		880
		Oct 1 Balance	363

J Rimmer

	£		£
Dec 1 Balance	160	Dec 6 Bank	156
15 Sales	57	Disc. all'd	4
24 Sales	94	28 Returns in	11
		31 Balance	140
	311		311
Jan 1 Balance	140		

6 Explain the purpose of each of the following:

advice note	statement
despatch note	debit note
consignment note	credit note
invoice	delivery note

Questions 7, 8 and 9: use the Trial Balance extracts to produce Trading Accounts for the six months ended as at the Trial Balance dates.

---

7   Extract from Trial Balance of
W Cowie as at
30 September 19-1

	£	£
Purchases and sales	16 120	20 098
Returns inwards and outwards	338	650
Stock at 1 March 19-1	5 200	

Stock at 30 September 19-1 was £5850

---

8   Extract from Trial Balance of
C Gough as at
31 March 19-2

	£	£
Purchases and sales	22 320	27 828
Returns in and out	468	900
Stock at 1 Sept 19-1	7 200	

The stock on hand at 31 March 19-2 was valued at £8100

---

9   Extract from Trial Balance of
P Lamb as at
30 June 19-4

	£	£
Returns in and out	546	1 050
Stock at 1 Jan 19-4	8 400	
Purchases and sales	26 040	32 466

The stock on hand at 30 June 19-4 was valued at £9450

Assignment 3

(To meet objectives C2, G1, G2, G4)

Due to the success of the first year's operations, Brown Electrics engaged a second assistant and purchased another van. The tenant of the garage had thus to relinquish his tenancy. The employment of the second man enabled Brown to undertake various contract work, which was conducted on a credit basis. Domestic servicing was still done only for cash.

From the following information you are required to:

a Open the accounts in the books of Brown Electrics
b Enter the transactions for the month of March 19—3
c Balance the accounts and extract a Trial Balance as at 31 March 19—3
d Produce a Trading and Profit and Loss Account for the year ended 31 March 19—3 and a Balance Sheet as at that date
e Prepare a diagrammatic presentation of your own choice to compare an important aspect of this year and the previous year's trading

Cash Receipts for Servicing
March 19—3

Day	£	Day	£	Day	£	Day	£	Day	£
		7	114	14	128	21	144	28	105
1	73	8	116	15	121	22	124	29	123
2	94	9	105	16	129	23	118	30	114
3	102	10	99	17	132	24	120	31	137
4	98	11	122	18	136	25	106		

188

BROWN ELECTRICS

Trial Balance as at 28 February 19-3

	£	£
Capital		3 296
Drawings	2 672	
Wages	5 870	
Office cleaning	572	
Rent	1 040	
Vans	1 760	
Equipment	614	
Petrol and repairs	1 128	
Road tax and insurance	352	
Workshop insurance	230	
Postage	97	
Carriage in	271	
Telephone	203	
Window cleaner	38	
Heat and light	517	
Administration expenses	1 358	
Basetshire Council	764	
Lewis, Jones & Co	183	
C Hardy Ltd	285	
Whites Appliances Ltd		1 924
Electrical Supplies Ltd		637
Home Services Ltd		586
Electro-Parts Ltd		252
Domestic Appliance Co		717
Purchases	19 926	
Income from servicing		32 661
Stock at 1 April 19-2	1 170	
Returns in and out	326	418
Discounts	454	1 072
Bank	1 640	
Cash in hand	93	
	41 563	41 563

Stock on hand at 28 February 19-3: £3856

Mar 1 Paid the following suppliers by cheque, deducting 5% cash discount in each case: Whites Appliances Ltd £900, Domestic Applicance Co £500

2 Received cheques from the following, allowed them $2^1/_2$% cash discount: Lewis, Jones & Co £160, C Hardy Ltd £200

3 Paid by cash: office cleaner £11 and assistants' wages £112; servicing on credit for C Hardy Ltd £240

4 Paid rent to Numac Co by cheque £20, and postage by cash £2.60; bought spares on credit from Electrical Supplies Ltd £270, less 15% trade discount

7 Paid cash for petrol £39

8 Bought stock items on credit from Home Services Ltd £155, less 20% trade discount

9 Returned faulty parts to Electrical Supplies Ltd £17

10 Paid by cash: office cleaner £11 and assistants' wages £112; bought items on credit from Domestic Applicance Co £320, less 20% trade discount

11 Paid rent by cheque to Numac Co £20; withdrew £87 from the till for private use; paid postage by cash £3.40; transferred £500 from Cash to Bank Account

14 Paid the following by cheque, in each case deducting 5% cash discount: Electrical Supplies £620, Home Services £586, Electro-Parts Ltd £252

15 Received cheque from Basetshire Council in settlement of full debt, allowed 5% cash discount; paid window cleaner by cash £4.50

16 Paid cash £178 for spare parts; paid 'phone bill by cheque £77

17 Paid cash: office cleaner £11 and assistants' wages £112

18 Paid for National Health stamps £58 cash; withdrew £87 cash for own use; paid petrol by cash £59

21 Servicing on credit for Basetshire Council £98; paid rent to Numac Co by cheque £20

22 Bought stock items on credit from Home Services £180, less 20% trade discount; paid for carriage inwards by cash £14

23 Paid electricity bill by cheque £212; paid postage by cash £7.40

24 Cash payments to office cleaner £11 and assistants' wages £112
25 Cash withdrawn for own use £83; rent paid to Numac Co £20 by cheque; petrol bill paid by cash £73; transferred from Cash to Bank Account £366.60
28 Bought spares on credit from Whites Appliances Ltd £340, less 20% trade discount
29 Basetshire Council returned faulty appliance £112
30 Servicing on credit for Lewis, Jones & Co £83
31 Paid by cash: office cleaner £11, assistants' wages £112; paid Numac Co by cheque for administrative expenses £136; withdrew £90 cash for own use; £400 cash was banked.

Note: Stock on hand valued at £4560.

14 Prepayments and accruals

Unit 6 showed how net profit was calculated by setting the period's expenses against the same period's income. Problems arise, however, when expenses for a period remain unpaid at the end of that period. Some expenses are payable in arrears, and it is not always the case that the period covered by the payments will be the same as that covered by the accounts. For example, electricity may be paid for after it has been consumed.

Suppose that Numac Trading Co's financial year ends on 31 December, whilst the quarter's electricity bill – payable in arrears – arrives at the beginning of the following February. The bill covers the period November, December and January.

From page 192 it can be seen that the bill covers two months of accounting period 1 and one month of accounting period 2. In order to set expenses against period 1's income, some allowance must be made for the electricity which has been used during November and December. In other words, an allowance must be made for the expenses outstanding at the end of the accounting period. Such outstanding expenses are sometimes called **accruals** or **expenses accrued**. They should be included in the Profit and Loss Account, where they are added to the expenses actually paid.

If the half yearly payment for electricity had been £500 with a further £100 still owing, the Profit and Loss Account entry would be as below.

These expenses owing also form some kind of liability for the firm; they are debts owed by the firm, and as such they should be listed in the Balance Sheet under 'current liabilities'.

```
          Extract from Profit & Loss Account
                      £     £
Electricity         500
Add Owing           100
                   -----
                          600
```

SOUTH MIDLANDS ELECTRICITY BOARD

Central Accounting Office   Electricity House   Summerhampton

Messrs Numac Trading Co
Norton Estate
Nottingham

VAT Reg. No: 238 5679 32
Consumer Ref. No: 3775 052

Tariff Code	Meter Reading		Units Used	Price Per Unit (p)	Quarterly Charges £	VAT Rate %	£
	Present	Previous					
8	46071	35761	10310	2.8613	5.00	0	300.00

Reading Date	Date of Issue of this Account		Amount Due Now
31.1.19-1	5.2.19-1		300.00

Prepayments

Similarly, some expenses are payable in advance: rent, rates and insurance are common examples. Payment must be made before the benefits can be enjoyed. Again, it is unlikely that the period covered by the payment will, in all cases, precisely match the period covered by the Profit and Loss Account. Following the rule that the period's expenses must be set against income for the period, it will be necessary to deduct that portion of the expenses which applies to a later period. These expenses are referred to as **prepayments**, and they should be deducted from the expenses in the Profit and Loss Account.

Hence, if the insurance payment this period covers some of the next accounting period, the Profit and Loss entry would be as follows.

Extract from Profit & Loss Account		
	£	£
Insurance	1 200	
Less Prepaid	200	
		1 000

In the Balance Sheet, prepayments are listed with current assets. They usually appear after 'debtors', since the person who has been paid is a particular type of debtor. The firm has paid for some benefit which it has not wholly received. In the case of insurance, the insurance company is liable for the unexpired term of the policy, while in the case of rates, the local authority owes its services to the firm for the unexpired time of the rate payment.

Prepayments and accruals usually appear as notes to the Trial Balance. Where they do, the basic rules are:

Prepayments are ~~added to~~ deducted from. expenses in the Profit and Loss Account and are included as current assets in the Balance Sheet

Accruals are ~~deducted from~~ added to expenses in the Profit and Loss Account and are included as current liabilities in the Balance Sheet.

Sometimes, the ledger accounts will already have dealt with the outstanding expenses or the prepayments. In these cases, the Trial Balance will contain an item such as 'rent prepaid'. The only requirement here is to list the expense in the Balance Sheet. No entry is necessary in the Profit and Loss Account, since the ledger accounts have already been amended.

If Numac had paid rent of £1700 during 19−5 of which £200 was for part of 19−6, the accounts would appear as below. The prepaid element − the £200 − is transferred to the debit side of the Rent Prepaid Account, signifying a special sort of debtor. The rent applicable to 19−5 is only £1500, and this is the amount actually transferred to 19−5 Profit and Loss Account.

```
                            Rent Paid
                     £                                    £
Jan   1  Bank        500     Dec 31  Rent
May   1  Bank        500             prepaid    200
Sept  1  Bank        700             Profit
                                     & Loss   1 500

                   ─────                                ─────
                   1 700                                1 700
                   ═════                                ═════

                          Rent Prepaid
                     £
Dec 31  Rent
        paid         200

            Extract from Profit & Loss Account
                     £
Rent               1 500
```

If no Rent Prepaid Account had been used, the information concerning prepayment would have appeared as a note to the Trial Balance, and the entries would have been as shown opposite.

```
                         Rent Paid
                    £                              £
   Jan  1 Bank      500    Dec 31  Profit
   May  1 Bank      500            & Loss  1 700
   Sept 1 Bank      700
                  _____                       _____
                  1 700                        1 700
                  ======                       ======


          Extract from Profit & Loss Account
                    £
   Rent         1 700
   Less
   Prepaid       200
                _____
                        1 500
```

Note that in either case, £1500 rent is set against the period's income.

A ledger account for the outstanding expense might also be used with accruals. If Numac had created an account for power bills accrued, showing that £4500 had been paid, but that £500 was still outstanding, the account would appear as shown at the top of page 196. Below it is shown the presentation which would be used if no accrued account were created and the accrual had appeared merely as a note to the Trial Balance.

Again, each method of presentation results in the same Profit and Loss Account figure.

In order to bring together the points made in this unit, and to revise items covered earlier, the following example is worked through. Study the steps carefully. The Trading and Profit and Loss Accounts and the Balance Sheet are presented in vertical form. The task is to produce the Trading and Profit and Loss Accounts for the three months ended 30 September and a Balance Sheet as at this date.

Extract from Profit & Loss Account

	£
Power	5 000

Power

	£		£
Jan 3 Bank	1 000	Dec 31 Profit	
May 4 Bank	1 500	& Loss	5 000
Sept 2 Bank	2 000		
Dec 31 Power accrued	500		
	5 000		5 000

Power Bills Accrued

		£
	Dec 31 Power	500

Extract from Profit & Loss Account

	£	£
Power	4 500	
Add		
Owing	500	
		5 000

Power

	£		£
Jan 3 Bank	1 000	Dec 31 Profit	
May 4 Bank	1 500	& Loss	4 500
Sept 2 Bank	2 000		
	4 500		4 500

By this stage you should be able to distinguish between the purchases and sales figures, returns inwards and returns outwards, debtors and creditors. Note that the item for wages owing appears within the Trial Balance, as does insurance prepaid. See how these are handled in the Profit and Loss Account, and compare them with the treatment of rates and telephone expenses.

```
                  NUMAC TRADING CO
       Trial Balance as at 30 September 19-1

                                    £           £
Capital                                      150 960
Drawings                        5 340
Advertising                     4 720
Postage                           810
Light and heat                  1 240
Wages                          49 500
Wages owing                                    1 260
Rates                           1 800
Telephone                       1 210
Motor expenses                  3 200
Insurance                       1 300
Insurance prepaid                  60
Premises                      127 000
Equipment                      10 000
Vans                           12 800
Furniture                       4 300
Purchases and sales           111 520     200 920
Returns in and out                420       1 620
Debtors and creditors          19 000      16 380
Bank                            9 220
Cash                              700
Stock at 1 July 19-1            7 000
                              ───────     ───────
                              371 140     371 140
                              ═══════     ═══════


Notes
1  Stock at 30 September 19-1 £3800.
2  £100 of rates refers to the following period.
3  Telephone bills for this quarter are £40
   outstanding.
```

NUMAC TRADING CO

Trading and Profit and Loss Accounts
for the three months ending
30 September 19-1

	£	£	£
Sales		200 920	
Less Returns in		420	
			200 500
Less Opening stock		7 000	
Purchases	111 520		
Less Returns out	1 620		
		109 900	
		116 900	
Less Closing stock		3 800	
Cost of goods sold			113 100
Gross profit			87 400
Less Advertising		4 720	
Postage		810	
Light and heat		1 240	
Wages		49 500	
Rates	1 800		
Less Prepaid	100		
		1 700	
Telephone	1 210		
Add Owing	40		
		1 250	
Motor expenses		3 200	
Insurance		1 300	
			63 720
Net profit			23 680

Study the presentation of prepayments and accruals within the Balance Sheet.

```
                    NUMAC TRADING CO
           Balance Sheet as at 30 September 19-1

                      £        £        £        £
   Assets employed

   Fixed assets
   Premises                           127 000
   Equipment                           10 000
   Vans                                12 800
   Furniture                            4 300
                                               154 100

   Current assets
   Stock                       3 800
   Debtors                    19 000
   Prepayments:
   Rates             100
   Insurance          60
                     ---
                               160
   Bank                       9 220
   Cash                         700
                              ------   32 880

   Less Current
   liabilities
   Creditors                  16 380
   Accruals:
   Wages            1 260
   Telephone           40
                    -----
                             1 300
                             ------   17 680
   Working capital                              15 200
                                               -------
                                               169 300
                                               =======

   Financed by:
   Capital                    150 960
   Add Net profit              23 680
                             --------
                                      174 640
   Less Drawings                        5 340
                                      -------
                                              169 300
                                              =======
```

Summary

On completion of this unit plus practice at the exercises you should be able to:

1 Explain the purpose of prepayments and accruals.
2 Describe the effect of prepayments and accruals on the profit calculation, and on the Balance Sheet.
3 Record prepayments and accruals in the accounting records.

Exercises

1 Explain the significance of each of the entries in the following accounts.

Rent

			£					£
Mar	1	Bank	1 500	Dec	31	Profit		
June	1	Bank	1 500			& Loss		5 000
Sept	1	Bank	1 500			Balance		1 000
Dec	1	Bank	1 500					
			6 000					6 000
Jan	1	Balance	1 000					

Salaries

			£					£
Mar	25	Bank	2 000	Dec	31	Profit		
June	24	Bank	2 600			& Loss		10 000
Sept	29	Bank	2 600					
Dec	24	Bank	2 600					
Dec	31	Balance	200					
			10 000					10 000
				Jan	1	Balance		200

2   Why are prepayments listed with assets in the Balance Sheet, whilst accruals are listed as liabilities?

3   What is the justification for adjusting the Profit and Loss Account to include prepayments and accruals?

4   The YZ Co ended its financial year on 31 December. In 19−1 the firm paid its rates by cheque £320 on 1 March and £340 on 1 September. Show the Rates Account as it would appear in YZ's books as at 31 December 19−1, when the necessary transfers had been made to the Profit and Loss Account.

5   During the year ended 31 March 19−3, D Day paid out £4080 cash in wages to his assistants. This represented wages for 51 weeks. At the close of business on 31 March 19−3, the week's wages was still owing to the assistants. Show the Wages Account as it would appear in Day's books as at 31 March 19−3, after the necessary transfers had been made to the Profit and Loss Account.

Questions 6−10: you are required to produce Trading and Profit and Loss Accounts for the periods ended as at the Trial Balance date, and a Balance Sheet as at that date.

6   Trial Balance of G Dawes
              as at 31 March 19-5

	£	£
Purchases and sales	29 663	40 670
Stock at 1 Sept 19-4	7 236	
Postage and telephone	399	
Motor expenses	823	
Motor expenses owing		38
Wages and salaries	7 637	
Rent and rates	683	
Rent prepaid	47	
Packing expenses	271	
Sundry expenses	145	
Debtors and creditors	8 222	5 689
Premises	17 500	
Motor vehicles	4 113	
Furniture and fittings	1 960	
Bank		2 552
Capital		36 488
Drawings	6 738	
	85 437	85 437

Notes at 31 March 19-5:
1 Stock: £5003
2 Prepayments: packing £21
3 Accruals: sundry expenses £25

```
7              Trial Balance of J Cliffe
               as at 30 September 19-3

                                      £         £
Purchases and sales             54 634    89 225
Returns                            756        521
Capital                                    43 418
Drawings                         5 292
Stock at 1 Oct 19-2             10 443
Wages                           16 275
Fuel and power                   2 222
Rent and rates                   1 686
Postage and telephone              344
Motor expenses                   2 927
Discounts                          882     1 544
Premises                        28 350
Vehicles                         1 638
Fixtures and fittings            1 544
Debtors and creditors           17 184     7 640
Cash at bank                               2 310
Cash in hand                       481
                                _____   _____
                               144 658   144 658
                                =======   =======
```

Notes at 30 September 19-3:
1 Stock £11 008
2 Prepayments: fuel and power £38,
             rent and rates £58
3 Accruals: wages £325, motor expenses £23.

8   Trial Balance of R Wynne
             as at 31 December 19-1

	£	£
Capital		31 380
Drawings	3 360	
Stock at 1 Jan 19-1	6 630	
Purchases and sales	34 689	56 650
Returns	480	330
Wages and salaries	10 334	
Rates and insurance	1 411	
Cleaning expenses	218	
Discounts	560	980
Motor expenses	1 859	
Office expenses	605	
Light and heat	465	
General expenses	879	
Premises	14 000	
Motor vehicles	5 040	
Furniture and fittings	980	
Debtors and creditors	10 910	4 850
Cash at bank	1 770	
	94 190	94 190

Notes at 31 December 19-1:
1 Stock: £6989
2 Expenses owing: office expenses £32
                    light and heat £64
3 Prepayments: insurance £57, rates £54.

9   Trial Balance of J Roseby
as at 31 March 19-3

	£	£
Capital		23 535
Drawings	2 520	
Stock at 1 April 19-2	4 973	
Purchases and sales	26 016	42 488
Returns	360	248
Wages and salaries	7 750	
Light and heat	1 058	
Rates	349	
Insurance	454	
Advertising	164	
Discounts	420	735
Motor expenses	1 394	
Administration expenses	659	
Premises	13 500	
Motor van	780	
Furniture	735	
Debtors and creditors	8 183	3 638
Cash at bank	1 100	
Cash in hand	229	
	70 644	70 644

Notes at 31 March 19-3:
1 Stock £5242
2 Prepayments: advertising £26, rates £32,
     insurance £32
3 Accruals: wages and salaries £705,
     administration expenses £71

10　　　　　Trial Balance of G Dove
as at 31 December 19-5

	£	£
Capital		58 995
Drawings	6 384	
Stock at 1 July 19-5	12 597	
Purchases and sales	65 909	98 135
Returns	912	627
Wages and salaries	19 635	
Rates and insurance	2 681	
Cleaning expenses	414	
Discounts	1 064	1 862
Motor expenses	3 532	
Office expenses	3 050	
Fuel and power	2 784	
Miscellaneous expenses	3 570	
Premises	20 216	
Motor vehicles	9 576	
Furniture and equipment	1 862	
Debtors and creditors	20 729	9 215
Bank		6 081
	174 915	174 915

Notes at 31 December 19-5:
1　Stock: £13279
2　Prepayments: rates £51, fuel £72
3　Accruals: wages £876, miscellaneous expenses £85

15 Provisions – bad debts and depreciation

Unit 14 showed how matching a period's expenses with the period's income can give rise to problems of prepayments and accruals. This basic principle of matching expenses and income can also cause other problems. Two of these concern debtors and fixed assets.

The list of assets on a Balance Sheet represents the value of the firm's possessions: assets are what a business owns. If these figures are to be useful to people who use the Balance Sheet, they should be reasonably realistic.

Bad debts

Consider the asset debtors. This asset represents the value of goods sold on credit for which payment is still awaited. The items have been sold in exchange for customers' promises to pay. If, for any reason, this promise is likely to be broken (i.e. if the customer is unlikely to pay) then the value of the asset is reduced. Clearly, if the Balance Sheet figures are to be a realistic reflection of the asset's value, then the figure for debtors must also be reduced.

Any customer who is unlikely to pay his debt has his account closed, and the outstanding amount is transferred to a Bad Debts Account. This account acts as a collection point for all the bad debts incurred during the period. At the end of the period, the total of the Bad Debts Account is transferred to the debit side of the Profit and Loss Account. This effectively increases the total of expenses, and thus reduces the total of net profit.

Assume that D Dewy and F Day owe Numac £50 and £30 respectively. Dewy has been declared bankrupt and his creditors are to receive nothing, whilst Day has left the area, and it is unlikely that his debt will ever be paid.

If these two accounts were to remain in the ledger as assets, the ledger would not be providing a realistic picture of the firm's financial standing. Far from possessing an asset, debtors, valued at £80, the firm has in fact incurred a loss of £80. The two debtors' accounts are therefore closed, and the outstanding balances transferred to the Bad Debts Account as shown opposite.

At the end of the period, the firm shows a loss of £80 on the Bad Debts Account instead of assets of £80 on the debtors' accounts. All other bad debts for the period amounted to a further £120. These bad debts along with Dewy's and Day's are transferred to the Profit and Loss Account as one total figure of £200.

Doubtful debts

Bad debts are those which are almost certain not to be paid. The customers and the amounts can be easily identified, and the accounts can be dealt with as above.

However, based on experience, most firms realise that their total figure for good debts at the end of a period includes a proportion of debts which will not be paid. The firm is unable to pinpoint exactly which customers will default: it merely knows that some will. In the light of this, it is not realistic to leave the figure for debtors unaltered. Some attempt must be made to adjust the asset to a proper level. This is done by creating a doubtful debts provision.

A **provision** involves allocating a proportion of the profits to cover a known liability which is of an unknown amount. Hence, with doubtful debts, the firm knows from past experience that a certain proportion of debts will not be honoured. It does not know, however, exactly what this proportion is likely to be.

Note also, that a provision is an allocation of *profits* and not of *cash*. Provisions do not improve a firm's financial standing: they merely help to provide a more realistic picture of what is happening.

In the year 19−2, Numac's total debtors, after deducting bad debts, were £36000. From past experience, the firm estimated that possibly 5% of these debts would not be paid. It was therefore decided to create a doubtful debts provision of 5% of debtors.

D Dewy

	£			£
Jan 1 Balance	50	June 1 Bad debts		50

F Day

	£			£
Jan 1 Balance	30	July 1 Bad debts		30

Bad Debts

	£			£
June 1 D Dewy	50	Dec 31 Profit & Loss		200
July 1 F Day	30			
	. . .			
	200			200

Extract from Profit & Loss Account

	£
Bad debts	200

The entries necessary to record this are quite straightforward. The Doubtful Debts Provision Account is credited with £1800 − 5% of £36000 − and the Profit and Loss Account is debited with the £1800. The effect of the entry on the Profit and Loss Account is to increase the amount of expenses to be set against the gross profit, and thus decrease the figure for net profit.

Doubtful Debts Provision		
		£
	Dec 31 Profit & Loss	1 800

Extract from Profit & Loss Account			
	£		£
Doubtful debts provision	1 800	Gross profit	xx

The £1800 credit balance on the Doubtful Debts Provision Account appears as a deduction from the debtors in the Balance Sheet.

Extract from Balance Sheet as at 31 December 19-2		
	£	£
Current assets		
Stock		xx
Debtors	36 000	
Less Provision	1 800	
		34 200
Bank		xx
Cash		xx

Suppose that in 19−3 the amount of Numac's debtors increases to £42000. The 5% provision would need to be £2100. However, the provision account already shows a figure of £1800 from the previous year, so all that is necessary is to increase it by £300.

```
                Doubtful Debts Provision
                      £                                    £
19-3                            19-3
Dec 31 Balance      2 100       Jan  1 Balance        1 800
                                Dec 31 Profit
                                       & Loss           300

                    2 100                             2 100

                                19-4
                                Jan  1 Balance        2 100

           Extract from Profit & Loss Account
                      £                                    £
Doubtful debts                  Gross profit             xx
provision           300
```

The Profit and Loss Account is thus debited with £300 and the provision account is credited with £300. The total of the Doubtful Debts Provision Account is now £2100, and this is the figure which is deducted from debtors in the Balance Sheet.

```
Extract from Balance Sheet as at 31 December 19-3
                                        £         £
Current assets
Stock                                            xx
Debtors                               42 000
Less Provision                         2 100

                                                39 900
Bank                                             xx
Cash                                             xx
```

In 19−4 Numac's debtors are £40000. A 5% provision would need to be £2000. However, the existing provision account shows a balance of £2100. It is necessary, therefore, to reduce the provision by £100. This is done by debiting the provision account by £100, and crediting the Profit and Loss Account with £100.

The balance on the provision account is thus reduced to the desired figure, and 19−4's net profit will be increased by £100. The Balance Sheet entry for debtors is again reduced by the *balance* on the provision account i.e. £2000.

Note that provision accounts always have credit balances, and it is these balances, and not the amendments, which appear in the Balance Sheet. The *amendments* appear in the Profit and Loss Account, but the *balances* appear in the Balance Sheet.

Doubtful Debts Provision

	£		£
19-4		19-4	
Dec 31 Profit		Jan 1 Balance	2 100
& Loss	100		
Balance	2 000		
	2 100		2 100
		19-5	
		Jan 1 Balance	2 000

Extract from Profit & Loss Account

	£
Gross profit	xx
Doubtful debts provision	100

Extract from Balance Sheet as at 31 December 19-4

	£	£
Current assets		
Stock		xx
Debtors	40 000	
Less Provision	2 000	
		38 000
Bank		xx
Cash		xx

Where, for any reason, the provision remains unaltered, no entry is required in the Profit and Loss Account, although in the Balance Sheet, the debtors figure is still reduced by the balance on the provision account.

Depreciation

Another known liability of an unknown amount is depreciation. **Depreciation** means a loss in value, and it applies mainly to reductions in the value of fixed assets. Depreciation can arise from many causes. The common ones are wear and tear, age and obsolescence.

For example, a motor car which has 40000 miles on the clock is likely to be worth less than a similar car with a recorded mileage of only 20000 miles. Similarly, even if the car has done only 10000 miles, if it is an out-of-date model for which spare parts are difficult to obtain, it will not have a high market value. So far as leases are concerned, a lease with 40 years to run will be worth more than one with only 10 years to run, provided all other considerations are similar.

If the Balance Sheet is to give a realistic picture of the value of the firm's fixed assets, some attempt must be made to measure this loss in value. The problem is a difficult one, since the only sure way to discover an item's value is to offer it for sale and see what it will fetch. Clearly, this approach is not acceptable.

There are well-organised markets for some second-hand assets, for example, property and vehicles. Where these markets exist, some guide to valuation can be obtained. Alternatively, expert valuers can be employed to give a professional opinion on an asset's worth. However, much industrial equipment is of a specialist nature, and assessing its value (other than as scrap) is not easy. Firms resolve the problem by using standard techniques for measuring depreciation. None of these methods gives an accurate assessment, but each operates along well-known lines, and they all go some way towards solving the difficulties.

By far the most popular method of calculating depreciation is the **straight line method**. This seeks to allocate against (i.e. deduct from) profits the same *absolute* amount, as a depreciation charge for each year of the asset's life. An alternative method (see Appendix C) seeks to allocate against profits the same *relative* amount each year.

The straight line method

The annual depreciation charge can be calculated simply by using the formula:

$$\frac{\text{Cost} - \text{Estimated Scrap Value}}{\text{Estimated Useful Life}}$$

Thus, if a lathe cost £8500, had an estimated useful life of 5 years, and a scrap value of £500 at the end of this period, the annual depreciation charge would be:

$$\frac{£8500 - £500}{5} = £1600$$

Depreciation is an expense, just as rent or rates are. As such, the depreciation charge must appear on the debit side of the Profit and Loss Account at the end of the period.

Since it is a liability of an uncertain amount, a Depreciation Provision Account is used to record the annual charge. Using the above example, the entries necessary to record the depreciation in the first year would be as follows:

Lathe			
19-1	£		
Jan 1 Bank	8 500		

Depreciation Provision			
19-1			£
		Dec 31 Profit	
		& Loss	1 600

Extract from Profit & Loss Account			
	£		£
Depreciation		Gross profit	xx
provision	1 600		

```
Extract from Balance Sheet as at 31 December 19-1
                                     £          £
Fixed assets
Lathe                              8 500
Less Depreciation                  1 600
                                   _____
                                              6 900
```

The provision account is credited with the depreciation charge of £1600, and the Profit and Loss Account is debited with £1600. In the Balance Sheet, the credit balance on the provision account is deducted from the asset: £8500 less £1600 gives £6900.

In the second year, a further £1600 would be written off in the Profit and Loss Account, this time against the second year's profit, and the Depreciation Provision Account would appear as below, the balance increasing by the second depreciation charge of £1600. Note that the Lathe Account remains unaltered. It does not change until the lathe is revalued or sold.

In 19−2's Balance Sheet, the asset would be reduced to £5300: £8500 less £3200, the accumulated depreciation to date.

```
                     Depreciation Provision
         _____
19-2                    £                                    £
Dec 31 Balance        3 200      Jan  1 Balance            1 600
                                 Dec 31 Profit
                                        & Loss            1 600
                      _____                              _____
                      3 200                               3 200
                      ======                              ======
19-3                             Jan  1 Balance           3 200
```

This annual depreciation would continue until the end of the fifth year, each year the balance on the provision account increasing by £1600, and the asset's value in the Balance Sheet diminishing by £1600. By the fifth year, the credit balance on the provision account will have reached £8000. The Balance Sheet will record the asset at its scrap value: £8500 less £8000 gives £500, and the asset will remain in the Balance Sheet at its scrap value until it is revalued or sold.

Depreciation Provision

19-5	£			£
Dec 31 Balance	8 000	Jan 1 Balance		6 400
		Dec 31 Profit		
		& Loss		1 600
	8 000			8 000
19-6		Jan 1 Balance		8 000

Extract from Balance Sheet as at 31 December 19-5

	£	£
Fixed assets		
Lathe	8 500	
Less Depreciation	8 000	
		500

Sale of assets

Obviously, since both the life of the asset and its scrap value are estimates, it is unlikely that the asset will depreciate exactly as calculated, or that it will be completely worn out at the end of its estimated life. For these reasons, if the asset is sold before the end of its estimated life, the firm is likely to find that it has either over- or under-depreciated.

Assume that the lathe is sold at the end of the second year for £6000 cheque. It is necessary to create a separate Sale of Asset Account to record this, since the sale of fixed assets does not feature in the Sales Account. (See opposite)

Lathe

19-2		£	19-2		£
Jan 1	Balance	8 500	Dec 31	Sale of asset	8 500

Depreciation Provision

19-2		£	19-2		£
Dec 31	Sale of asset	3 200	Dec 31	Balance	10 300
	Balance	7 100			
		10 300			10 300
			19-3		
			Jan 1	Balance	7 100

Sale of Asset

		£			£
Dec 31	Lathe	8 500	Dec 31	Deprecia-tion provision	3 200
	Profit & Loss (profit on sale)	700		Bank	6 000
		9 200			9 200

Extract from Profit & Loss Account 19-2

	£
Gross profit	xx
Profit on sale of asset	700

The Sale of Asset Account is used to bring together all those entries which relate to the asset being sold. Thus, the Lathe Account is closed and the £8500 transferred to the debit side of Sale of Asset Account. The Depreciation Provision Account is reduced by the amount of the provision which refers to the lathe. In this example, the Depreciation Provision Account refers solely to the lathe, but in reality the Depreciation Provision Account would record all depreciation charges for all those fixed assets which have been depreciated. Assuming that other assets have been depreciated so that the provision account has a balance of £10 300, £3200 of this applies to the lathe.

The £6000 cheque is entered on the credit side of the Sale of Asset Account, leaving the credit side of the account greater than the debit side. This difference of £700 represents the profit on the sale. It is the amount by which the lathe has been over-depreciated. This profit is transferred to the credit side of Profit and Loss Account for year 2, thus increasing the amount of net profit for that year.

If, however, the lathe was sold for £5000 cash, the Sale of Asset Account would appear as below. The Lathe Account, and the Depreciation Provision Account would remain as on page 217: only the Sale of Asset Account and the Profit and Loss Account would change.

	Sale of Asset				
		£			£
Dec 31 Lathe		8 500	Dec 31	Depreciation provision	3 200
				Cash	5 000
				Profit & Loss (loss on sale)	*300*
		8 500			8 500

	Extract from Profit & Loss Account 19-2		
		£		£
Loss on sale	*300*	Gross profit	xx

Selling the lathe at £5000 reveals that it was under-depreciated by £300. A loss of £300 is thus incurred when the lathe is sold. The loss is revealed on the credit side of the Sale of Asset Account, and it is transferred to the debit side of the Profit and Loss Account.

Note, therefore, that if the depreciation provision plus the sale price is *less* than the original cost, a *loss* is made on the sale. If the depreciation provision plus the sale price comes to *more* than the original cost, then a *profit* is made on the sale. Where the sale price plus the provision just equals the cost, then the correct amount of depreciation has been charged, and neither a profit nor a loss arises. In the example, if the lathe had been sold for £5300, the Sale of Asset Account would be as below showing neither profit nor loss. Again, the Lathe Account and the Depreciation Provision Account remain the same as on page 217.

Note, too, that where an asset is sold, it is removed from the list of fixed assets appearing in the Balance Sheet, thus reducing the total figure for fixed assets.

Sale of Asset				
	£			£
Dec 31 Lathe	8 500	Dec 31	Deprecia-tion provision	3 200
			Cash	5 300
	8 500			8 500

Summary

On completion of this unit plus practice at the exercises you should be able to:

1 Describe the reasons for creating provisions for doubtful debts and depreciation.
2 Record the accounting procedure for bad debts.
3 Record the accounting procedure for doubtful debt provisions and depreciation provisions.

220

Exercises

1 On 31 March 19−1, G Dawson decided to write off the following customers' debts as bad: B Hendy £47, C Drury £53, O Hobbs £28. Show the customers' accounts and the Bad Debts Account as they would appear after the above transaction.

2 Explain fully the significance of each of the following transactions:

	D Dando				
		£			£
Jan 31 Balance		420	Feb 4 Returns		15
			17 Bank		190
			Disc. all'd		10
			28 Balance		205
		420			420
Mar 1 Balance		205	Dec 31 Bad debts		205

	Bad Debts				
		£			£
Mar 31 C Cook		48	Dec 31 Profit		
June 30 I Dalwood		52	& Loss		147
Dec 31 A Bird		47			
		147			147

3 Why is it prudent to provide for doubtful debts?

4 What is the difference between writing off bad debts, and providing for doubtful debts?

5   M Shean provides for doubtful debts at 5% of debtors. In 19−1 his debtors were £8000, in 19−2 they were £10000 and in 19−3 they were £9000. Show the Doubtful Debts Provision Account for each of the 3 years.

6   Explain the meaning of each entry in the following account:

Doubtful Debts Provision			
	£		£
19-2 Balance	800	19-1 Profit & Loss	600
		19-2 Profit & Loss	200
	800		800
19-3 Profit & Loss	100	19-3 Balance	800
Balance	700		
	800		800
		19-4 Balance	700

7   On 1 January 19−1 Jones & Co purchased a new lathe costing £9850. The lathe was paid for by cheque. It was estimated that the lathe's useful life would be 8 years, at the end of which its estimated scrap value would be £250. Jones & Co use the straight line method of depreciation. Show
a the Lathe Account and
b the Depreciation Provision Account for the first 4 years. Jones' financial year ends on 31 December.
(Keep your answer; you will need it for Question 8).

8   Assume that Jones & Co sold the lathe in Question 7 at the end of the fourth year. Show the entries necessary to record the sale, assuming that the lathe was sold for cash at a price of:

a £5050
b £5800
c £4950

9   On 1 April 19−5, Chiswell & Sons purchased a new delivery van on credit from Central Garages Ltd for £3400. It was thought that Chiswells would keep the vehicle for 3 years, after which time it would be sold for £400. The firm uses the straight line method of depreciation. Show

a the entries necessary to record the purchase of the van, and
b the Depreciation Provision Account for each of the 3 years. Chiswell's financial year ends on 31 March.
(Keep your answer; you will need it for Question 10).

10   Assume that Chiswell & Sons sold the van in Question 9 on credit to T Young on 31 March 19−8. Show the entries necessary to record the sale, assuming that the price paid by Young was:

a £250
b £400
c £500

11   The following Sale of Asset Account appeared in the books of R Thomas. Explain the significance of each entry.

Sale of Asset			
	£		£
Dec 31 Equipment	2 700	Dec 31 C Ansoff	2 400
		Profit	
		& Loss	300
	2 700		2 700

Assignment 4

(To meet objectives A3, B2, B3, F1, G1, G3, G4, J2, J3)

On the following pages are the final accounts of Brown Electrics for the 11 months ending 28 February 19−3.

Brown's book-keeper has not provided for depreciation nor has he allowed for doubtful debts. It is agreed that the current worth of the vans is £1130, and the equipment, £570. A provision for doubtful debts is to be created at 2% of debtors, rounded to the nearest £.

Expenses outstanding at 28 February, for the 11 month period are: telephone £48, heat and light £74, wages £290. Expenses prepaid were: workshop insurance £27, road tax and insurance £64, administrative expenses £160.

You are required:

a to redraft Brown Electrics' accounts, showing the result of including the above items.
b Write a report to Brown's book-keeper, explaining why these alterations have been made even though his accounts balance without them, and their inclusion will reduce the figure for net profit.
c Present current assets as at 28 February 19−3 as a pie chart.
d Show on a semi-logarithmic graph, the servicing income and mileage logged from April 19−2 to February 19−3. Comment on your graph.

BROWN ELECTRICS

Trading and Profit & Loss Accounts
for the 11 months ended
28 February 19-3

	£	£	£	£
Revenue from servicing			32 661	
Less Returns in			326	
				32 335
Less Opening stock		1 170		
Purchases	19 926			
Less Returns out	418			
		19 508		
			20 678	
Less Closing stock			3 856	
				16 822
Gross profit				15 513
Discounts received				1 072
				16 585
Less Wages			5 870	
Office cleaning			572	
Rent			1 040	
Petrol			1 128	
Road tax and insurance			352	
Workshop insurance			230	
Postage			97	
Carriage			271	
Telephone			203	
Window cleaner			38	
Heat and light			517	
Administration expenses			1 358	
Discounts allowed			454	
				12 130
Net profit				4 455

BROWN ELECTRICS
Balance Sheet as at 28 February 19-3

	£	£	£
Assets employed:			
Fixed assets			
Vans		1 760	
Equipment		614	
			2 374
Current assets			
Stock	3 856		
Debtors	1 232		
Bank	1 640		
Cash	93		
		6 821	
Less Current liabilities			
Creditors		4 116	
Working capital			2 705
			5 079
Financed by:			
Capital	3 296		
Net profit	4 455		
		7 751	
Less Drawings		2 672	
			5 079

16 Interpretation of financial statements

So far, the manner in which accounting records are compiled has been studied along with the conventions used in recording business transactions. Now, ways in which these accounting statements can be used to help management decision-making will be examined.

Clearly, in an introductory text, this examination must necessarily be brief. One must also remember that managers are presented with information from numerous different sources other than the accounting system. Departments such as marketing, personnel, research and development will each be called upon to give their expert opinion on particular aspects of the firm's operations. One must remember, therefore, that whilst this unit is concerned with the interpretation of accounting statements, this is only one source of management information.

Neither is it only a firm's managers who are interested in the results of financial analysis. Those who supply funds to the firm will be interested; people such as creditors and those making extended loans. A firm's employees will also be interested, since they, too, have a stake in the firm's well being.

Of course, the information being sought by one group of people may well be different from that sought by another group. Creditors will be primarily concerned with the firm's ability to pay its debts, whilst the owner may be interested in the business's profits. Whoever the interested parties are, the starting point for analysis will invariably be the firm's Trading and Profit and Loss Accounts, and the Balance Sheet.

To simplify the discussion, only the 'final accounts': the Trading and Profit and Loss Accounts and the Balance Sheet will be used.

Financial ratios

Before beginning to measure performance, a yardstick is required. The most commonly used yardstick is a ratio which relates two pieces of financial information. Such ratios often convey vital information in a more meaningful way than does the raw data in financial statements.

Two types of comparison are possible in analysing financial ratios.

a time series analysis
b cross sectional analysis

In **time series analysis**, a firm's performance ratio for one period is compared with that same firm's ratios for previous periods. Trends can then be detected, and if necessary, action taken to influence the likely course of future events.

With **cross sectional analysis**, a particular firm's ratios may be compared with figures for the industry as a whole, to derive an idea of just how the firm compares with its competitors. Financial ratios for various industries are published regularly by such organisations as Dun and Bradstreet and the Centre for Interfirm Comparison. Some trade associations also publish financial ratios. Such specialist ratios are far more useful for comparison than the rule of thumb yardsticks so often adopted.

It is important to remember also that ratios are not ends in themselves. Ratios are produced in numerical form – often to two or three decimal places – so there is a danger that they will be regarded as a precise measure of performance. They are not precise measures however: they merely indicate where further analysis might usefully be carried out.

It has already been stated that items such as depreciation and doubtful debts provisions are simply estimates made by accountants in an effort to produce workable figures, and because they are estimates, they may not accurately reflect the real situation. It is necessary, therefore, to take care when using financial ratios.

When one considers the amount of information contained in a firm's final accounts, it is clear that a wide variety of ratios can be calculated. Some of the more important ratios are discussed below; in particular profitability and liquidity ratios.

Profitability ratios

The businessman will wish to know not simply what his gross profit is, but also what value of goods he has to sell in order to earn that profit. He will thus compare his gross profit with his sales. When profit is expressed as either a fraction of sales or as a percentage of sales it is referred to as the **profit margin**.

```
                  NUMAC TRADING CO
          Trading Account for the month ended
                  31 December 19-1

                        £                              £
Opening stock        5 200    Sales             65 000
Purchases           35 000
                    -------
                    40 200
Less Closing
     stock           6 000
                    -------
Cost of           · 34 200
goods sold
Gross profit        30 800
                    -------                        -------
                    65 000                         65 000
                    =======                        =======
```

Numac's Trading Account from Unit 7 is reproduced above. In order to calculate the profit margin, the gross profit must be expressed as a percentage of sales:

$$\frac{\text{Gross profit}}{\text{Sales}} \times 100 = \frac{30\ 800}{65\ 000} \times 100 = 47.38\%$$

This figure states that during December, Numac earned £47.38 profit for each £100 of sales. The margin is thus a measure of the profitability of sales.

Note that by simply increasing the value of sales, the gross profit will not automatically increase. Compare the above December figure with September; sales were some £7000 less in December and gross profit dropped from £31 300 to £30 800:

	Sept £	Dec £		Sept £	Dec £
NUMAC TRADING CO					
Monthly Trading Accounts 19-1					
Stock	4 500	5 200	Sales	72 000	65 000
Purchases	40 000	35 000			
	44 500	40 200			
Less Stock	3 800	6 000			
Cost of goods sold	40 700	34 200			
Gross profit	31 300	30 800			
	72 000	65 000		72 000	65 000

The ratios, however, show a different picture.

September $\dfrac{31\ 300}{72\ 000} \times 100 = 43.47$ per cent

December $\dfrac{30\ 800}{65\ 000} \times 100 = 47.38$ per cent

Note the difference between the two ratios. Although sales fell in December, the ratio improved and actual gross profit was only £500 less.

There may be a number of reasons for such a difference in the percentage. The sales mix may have changed, so that more items have been sold with a low profit margin than items with a high profit margin. The cost of the goods may have increased, whilst the selling price has remained unchanged. Again, perhaps the firm has reduced selling prices in order to stimulate sales. Alternatively, the amount of wastage may have increased significantly, and so might the amount of pilfering.

The figures themselves do not show the reason; they simply warn that something has changed. It is now up to Numac's management to investigate and see what has happened.

An opportunity to examine relationships over a period of time can be achieved by using a **scatter diagram**. This form of presentation enables one variable to be placed on one axis and the other variable on the other axis. It is not important on this type of graph to determine which is the dependent variable and which is the independent; it would often be difficult to do so anyway.

By using the two variables discussed above i.e. sales and gross profit, a scale is provided on each axis for the range of the variables used. Using Numac's figures for sales and gross profit shown on page 103 (reproduced below for reference) for July to December, create a scale on the X-axis for sales from 61400 to 75900 and a scale on the Y-axis for gross profit from 27400 to 35300. Then plot the intersection of gross profit and sales for each month.

	July	Aug	Sept	Oct	Nov	Dec
Sales	61400	67100	72000	75900	70000	65000
Gross profit	27400	28700	31300	35300	32700	30800

The scatter diagram is shown completed on page 231.

The value of scatter diagrams is that they show relationships between two sets of variables. They do not provide an opportunity for measurement, but it will be noticed that the graph below gives a pattern of plots which is rising. This pattern is a positive relationship

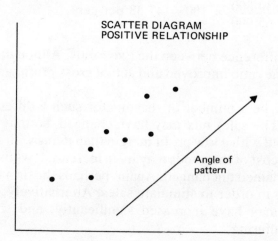

SCATTER DIAGRAM
POSITIVE RELATIONSHIP

Angle of
pattern

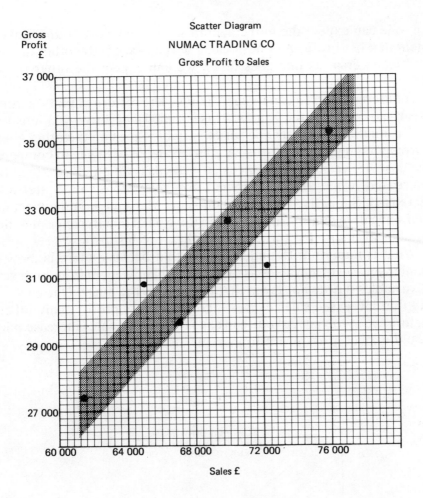

Scatter Diagram

NUMAC TRADING CO

Gross Profit to Sales

Gross Profit £

Sales £

i.e. one can expect the movement in sales to be close to the movement in gross profit. As one goes up we can expect the other to rise and vice versa, as one goes down we can expect the other to go down.

A different pattern can be seen below. The pattern of plots is from the Y-axis down to the X-axis. This is called a negative relationship i.e. a situation where as one set of variables goes up the other goes correspondingly downwards. A good example of this is to compare the last 15 years' attendances at cinemas which have steadily decreased while licences issued for televisions have steadily increased. Similarly, Numac's Transport Manager would expect to find a negative relationship between the cost of maintenance and the number of hours lost through breakdown of his lorries.

What is important to understand is that because there is movement in one set of variables associated with movement in another set of variables it does *not* mean that one causes the other. One cannot say that increased sales causes increased gross profit; many other factors are involved. All one can say is that when sales increase one would expect gross profit to increase as well.

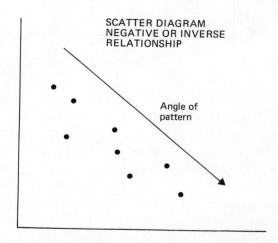

SCATTER DIAGRAM
NEGATIVE OR INVERSE
RELATIONSHIP

Angle of
pattern

There will be many occasions when there is no relationship between two sets of variables, in which case the plots will not show any particular pattern. This is illustrated below.

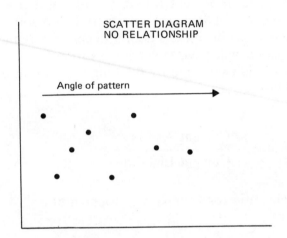

SCATTER DIAGRAM
NO RELATIONSHIP

Angle of pattern

Liquidity ratios

Liquidity is the ability to change an item of value into money. Since the firm has to pay its own debts in money, it must therefore be capable of converting its assets into cash in order to do this.

Remember that on the Balance Sheet, current assets are listed in order of permanence with the more permanent – and thus less liquid – items first. Hence, current assets are listed in the order of stock, debtors, bank and cash, progressing from the least liquid to the most liquid.

It is important that a firm is able to pay its short-term debts – in other words, its current liabilities – easily from its short-term assets. Those people, such as banks and trade creditors, who lend money to a business will be particularly interested in a firm's ability to pay its debts. Since liquidity ratios are a measure of this ability, they will be of particular interest to these groups of people.

Current ratio

The **current ratio** seeks to compare a firm's short-term assets with its short-term liabilities, since it is from the former that the latter are to be paid. A firm that has to sell or mortgage its fixed assets in order to pay its short-term debts is likely to be in severe financial trouble, since fixed assets represent the very basis of a firm's ability to generate revenue. If a haulage firm has to sell off some of its lorries to pay its debts, the business's ability to earn future income will be lessened, since it will have fewer lorries to put on the road.

Current ratio is calculated by dividing the current assets by the current liabilities:

$$\text{Current Ratio} = \frac{\text{Current Assets}}{\text{Current Liabilities}}$$

The current ratio for Company A (opposite) is:

$$\frac{10\ 440}{5\ 800} = 1.8$$

This means that the current assets are 1.8 times greater than the current liabilities i.e. £5800 × 1.8 = £10 440. The firm is thus capable of paying off its current liabilities from its current assets.

A quick rule of thumb is that the current assets should be twice the figure of the current liabilities for a healthy liquidity position. A ratio of much less than this indicates that the firm might have difficulty in paying its debts, whilst a firm which has too high a current ratio probably has too much of its funds tied up in current assets. It might, therefore, be losing profitable investment opportunities. After all, debtors, bank and cash items do not earn profit.

The rule that the current ratio should be about 2:1 is only very general. Many successful companies operate with ratios of less than this. Much depends upon the nature of the firm's business, and the time when the ratio is calculated. A firm which is collecting money just before undertaking a major investment programme is likely to be more liquid than normal.

Using two actual company reports, the Midland Educational Company Ltd in 1978 had current assets of £2 144 689 and current liabilities of £1 331 016 giving a current ratio of 1.61. Associated Television Corporation Ltd in 1978 had current assets of £75 914 000 and current liabilities of £51 982 000 giving a current ratio of 1.46.

The above two ratios show that companies can quite confidently exist on a figure of less than our rule of thumb guide of 2:1. The nature of a firm's business will affect the size of its ratio.

Balance Sheet extracts					
	Co A	Co B		Co A	Co B
	£	£		£	£
Current liabilities	5 800	5 800	Current assets		
			Stocks	2 400	5 210
			Debtors	4 350	4 100
			Bank	1 690	1 000
			Cash	2 000	130
	5 800	5 800		10 440	10 440

The current ratio's basic assumption − that the higher the ratio, the greater the firm's ability to pay its creditors − is open to other interpretations. The ratio does not take into account the liquidity of individual items which make up the current assets.

Cash in the bank and cash in hand are more liquid assets than stocks, since stocks must be sold before their value can be converted into cash. The items cash and bank, on the other hand, are already in cash form. Thus, a firm whose current assets are composed primarily of cash is far more able to pay its debts than a firm whose current assets are primarily stocks.

In the Balance Sheets shown above, both firms have the same current ratio of 1.8, but the composition of the current assets is markedly different, as is their ability to pay their creditors. Clearly, some other ratio is needed to distinguish the two situations.

Quick ratio

The **quick ratio** — sometimes called the acid test ratio, or the quick asset ratio — seeks to measure a firm's liquidity by excluding from the calculation the least liquid of the current assets. Thus, the quick ratio omits the stock figure from the total of current assets, and concentrates on the more liquid items of debtors, bank and cash. In this way, some distinction can be made between firms with high stock figures and those with low stock figures.

$$\text{Quick Ratio} = \frac{\text{Debtors} + \text{Prepayments} + \text{Bank} + \text{Cash}}{\text{Current Liabilities}}$$

Since prepayments are a form of debtor, they should be included in the calculation too.

In our example, although both firms have the same current ratio, they produce very different quick ratios.

Co A

$$\frac{4350 + 1690 + 2000}{5800} = \frac{8040}{5800} = 1.39$$

Co B

$$\frac{4100 + 1000 + 130}{5800} = \frac{5230}{5800} = 0.90$$

One can see that Co A is well able to pay off its current liabilities from its quick assets, whereas Co B has insufficient quick assets to satisfy its short-term creditors.

The general rule is that the quick ratio should be about 1:1 for a healthy liquidity position. Thus, the quick assets should just equal the current liabilities. In practice, ratios of less than this may be quite acceptable, but much depends on the type of business, and the confidence it enjoys with its creditors. Ratios of much less than 1:1 can indicate a dangerously illiquid position, and such ratios need investigation.

The Midland Educational Company Ltd in 1978, however, had quick assets of £522 994 and current liabilities of £1 331 016 giving a quick ratio of 0.39. Associated Television Corporation Ltd had quick assets of £34 598 000 and current liabilities of £51 982 000 giving a quick ratio of 0.66. This emphasises that companies of good standing can exist on a ratio of less than 1:1 and it is important not to jump to certain conclusions from isolated pieces of data.

Liquidity of debtors

The above examples illustrate that there may well be differences in the composition of a firm's current assets. Since these differences are significant, it may be useful to examine individually the various components of the current assets.

For instance, although debtors are listed as current assets, they may not in fact be of any financial value, since some of the debts may never be paid. Accountants allow for this in writing off the bad debts and providing for the doubtful ones.

A further problem arises in that some of the debts may not be current; some may be long overdue. To list such debts as liquid assets may be to mistake the true situation, since the firm may be unable readily to turn them into cash.

One method of analysing debtors is the **average collection period ratio**. This ratio shows the number of days that debts are outstanding: the average time it takes to turn them into cash. The ratio is calculated as follows:

$$\text{Average Collection Period Ratio} = \frac{\text{Debtors} \times 365}{\text{Annual Sales}}$$

Strictly speaking, only total credit sales figures ought to be used, but this figure is rarely available, so the figure for total annual sales is used instead.

The answer obtained should be compared with the terms offered by the firm to its credit customers. Assume that the firm's debtors at the end of the year total £6575, and that sales for the year were £60000.

The ratio is then calculated:

$$\frac{6575 \times 365}{60\,000} = 40$$

If the company's terms are such that outstanding debts should be paid within 30 days, and the average collection period is 40 days, then the indication is that many debts are long overdue. However, if the average collection period is 28 days, then it appears that most debts are being paid before they fall due.

Once again, having considered the theory, the principle should be applied to our two real companies. The Midland Educational Co Ltd at the end of their financial year had a turnover of £7 527 704 and a figure of £474 617 for debtors and prepayments. Unfortunately, the extent of prepayments included in this figure is not shown, but for the sake of calculation assume that the total is wholly debtors. Thus the average collection period ratio is:

$$\frac{\text{Debtors} \times 365}{\text{Annual Sales}}$$

$$\frac{474\,617 \times 365}{7\,527\,704} = 23 \text{ days}$$

In 1977 the figure was 22.7. The 1978 figure is not surprising since much of the business is cash sales of books and stationery.

Associated Television Corporation Ltd in 1978 had debtors and payments in advance, of £28 278 000 and a turnover of £113 588 000. (The extent of prepayments will again be ignored). Thus:

$$\frac{28\,278\,000 \times 365}{113\,588\,000} = 90 \text{ days}$$

Obviously, the making of films and longer-term contracts make the collection of debts more difficult to enforce on a 30 day basis. These two examples reinforce the point that ratios need to be studied carefully and related to the business of the company.

Liquidity of stocks

The size of a firm's gross profit will depend upon how quickly stocks are sold, since it is only when items are sold and the money received that a profit is actually made. The quicker stocks are sold i.e. are converted into cash, the greater will be the amount of profit earned.

The **rate of turnover** or **rate of stock turn** is a measure of the liquidity of stocks. It measures how quickly stocks can be turned into cash. The formula is as follows:

$$\text{Rate of Turnover} = \frac{\text{Cost of Goods Sold}}{\text{Average Stock}}$$

For practical purposes, the average stock figure is calculated by adding opening and closing stocks for a period and dividing the result by two.

```
                    NUMAC TRADING CO
          Trading Account for month ended
                  30 September 19-1
                      £                              £
Opening stock      4 500     Sales            72 000
Purchases         40 000
                  ───────
                  44 500
Less Closing
     stock         3 800
                  ───────
Cost of
goods sold        40 700
Gross profit      31 300
                  ───────                      ───────
                  72 000                        72 000
                  ═══════                       ═══════
```

In the above Trading Account, the average stock figure is

calculated using the formula:

$$\frac{\text{Opening Stock} + \text{Closing Stock}}{2}$$

$$= \frac{4500 + 3800}{2}$$

$$= \frac{8300}{2}$$

$$= 4150$$

The rate of turnover is thus:

$$\frac{\text{Cost of Goods Sold}}{\text{Average Stock}}$$

$$= \frac{40\ 700}{4\ 150}$$

$$= 9.81$$

This figure should then be compared with similar figures for previous months, or with figures produced by similar firms. The higher the figure, the faster the rate of turnover and the greater the liquidity of the stocks.

Using the two examples of company accounts, the rate of turnover for the Midland Educational Co Ltd was as follows: closing stock at the end of March 1977 was £1 450 029 and at the end of March 1978, £1 621 695. Thus the average stock figure is £1 535 862. Turnover for the year was £7 527 704 which gives a rate of turnover of:

$$\frac{7\ 527\ 704}{1\ 535\ 862}$$

$$= 4.90$$

The rate of turnover for the previous year was 4.5, so 1977 showed some improvement.

Associated Television Corporation Ltd, in a totally different line of business had average stocks of £5 147 000 and a turnover of £113 588 000. The rate of turnover was thus:

$$\frac{113\ 588\ 000}{5\ 147\ 000}$$

$$= 22.07$$

A television programme company is not selling stock, however; it is selling a service and its real assets are its people, so this particular ratio is not relevant here. Cadbury Schweppes Ltd will provide a more useful comparison. Cadbury Schweppes Ltd group sales for 1977 were £883.6 million and stock was, on average, £183.6 million, giving a rate of turnover of 4.8. The previous year it was 4.6, so stock turnover had improved.

Many other ratios can be calculated, and there are many other tools of analysis. The ratios discussed in this unit are the basic ones applicable to a wide variety of firms.

Summary

On completion of this unit plus practice at the exercises you should be able to:

1 Calculate from financial statements an organisation's profit margin, current ratio, quick asset ratio, liquidity of debtors and liquidity of stocks. (E2)
2 Explain the purposes of the above ratios and measurements. (E2)

Exercises
Towards objective E2

1 From the following Trading Accounts calculate:

a the percentage of gross profit to sales
b the rate of stock turnover

Comment on your results.

```
           WELTON TRADING CO

            Trading Accounts
          for years 19-1 and 19-2
                         19-1          19-2
                          £             £
        Sales           87 860       105 432
                        ══════       ═══════

        Opening stock    8 600        10 500
        Purchases       67 600        86 437
                        ──────       ───────
                        76 200        96 937
        Closing stock   10 500        14 700
                        ──────       ───────
        Cost of goods sold 65 700     82 237
        Gross profit    22 160        23 195
                        ──────       ───────
                        87 860       105 432
                        ══════       ═══════
```

2 Numac employs two buyers for footwear and the Sales Director
produced the following data from the purchasing and sales records
of how each buyer's purchases had been selling in a particular
period.

Shoe size	3	4	5	6	7	8	9	10	11
Buyer A	22	14	17	26	17	19	30	25	17
Buyer B	25	18	12	25	23	16	35	28	19

Plot the two buyers' figures (one on each axis) in a scatter diagram
and determine whether there is any recognisable relationship between the two. (Objective B2)

3 Use the following information to calculate:

a the percentage of gross profit to sales
b the rate of stock turnover

Comment on your results.

```
            SOMERVALE SERVICES CO

               Trading Accounts
            for years 19-4 and 19-5
                        19-4            19-5
                         £               £
Sales                 156 800         133 280
                      =======         =======

Opening stock          13 200          14 800
Purchases             125 440          92 440

                      138 640         107 240
Closing stock          14 800           4 240

Cost of goods sold    123 840         103 000
Gross profit           32 960          30 280

                      156 800         133 280
                      =======         =======
```

4 Numac carried out an analysis of its sales for 19−1 and the distance of its customers' addresses from its warehouse. Construct a scatter diagram and comment on the relationship between distance and sales. (Objective B2)

Customers' address (miles from warehouse)	Sales to customers (£000)
25	200
50	180
75	160
100	85
125	45
150	15
175	40
200	5

5   The following information was taken from the books of Westfield Factors. Calculate such ratios as you think necessary, and on the basis of the information you have, discuss the firm's position as at the end of 19−3.

```
                     WESTFIELD FACTORS
             Balance Sheet extracts
                          19-1       19-2       19-3
                           £          £          £
Current liabilities
Creditors                8 560      9 230      9 215
Overdraft                                        270

Current assets
Stock                    9 416      8 768      6 166
Debtors                  5 755      7 214      7 021
Bank                     2 682      1 468        -
Cash                       123         86         92
```

6   The Census of Distribution for 1971 gave the following information

Employees per organisation	Purchases (£000)	Beg. of year stock (£000)	End of year stock (£000)
1	225 645	36 998	40 518
2 — 4	2 240 502	297 864	326 386
5 — 9	1 735 972	245 368	267 848
10 — 19	876 618	134 370	146 789
20 — 99	860 768	149 938	164 890
100 — 999	1 335 076	215 688	235 466
1000 — 9999	2 226 619	303 388	316 403
10 000 +	2 151 675	283 638	304 404

Calculate the rate of turnover for each category and draw some conclusions (assume cost of goods sold = purchases).

7   Using the information in the Balance Sheet below, write a report on the financial state of Norton Trading Co as at 31 March, 19—8.

```
                    NORTON TRADING CO
          Balance Sheet as at 31 March 19-8

                              £          £          £
Assets employed

Fixed assets
Premises and equipment                18 580
Less Accumulated
       depreciation                    6 900
                                                  11 680
Current assets
Stock                      10 368
Debtors                     6 722
Prepayments                    78
Cash                          112
                                      17 280
Less Current liabilities
Creditors                   6 948
Overdraft                   1 692
                                       8 640
Working capital                                    8 640
                                                  20 320
                                                  ======
Financed by:
Capital                                           28 650
Less Net loss                          2 720
     Drawings                          5 610
                                                   8 330
                                                  20 320
                                                  ======
```

Abstract from Census of Distribution 1971

Employees	1	2-4	5-9	10-19	20-99	100-999	1000-9999	10 000+
Organis- ations	56 506	198 122	69 763	19 796	6 955	996	200	18
Persons employed	56 506	540 222	437 995	255 427	234 532	299 281	494 245	455 306
Turnover (£000)	322 937	2 986 239	2 313 662	1 191 336	1 207 664	1 902 985	3 330 349	3 020 392
Purchases (£000)	225 645	2 240 502	1 735 972	876 618	860 768	1 335 076	2 226 619	2 151 675

Source: Census of Distribution 1971

8   Using the table opposite calculate the gross profit (turnover less purchases) and express this in absolute terms (the actual value). Express this gross profit as a percentage of turnover for each category. Draw some conclusions from your results. (Objective A3, J1)

9   Using the table opposite calculate the amount of turnover for each organisation within each category. Draw some conclusions from your results. (Objective A3, J1)

10   Using the table opposite calculate the amount of turnover per employee within each category. Draw some conclusions from your results. (Objectives A3, J1)

11   Using the table opposite calculate the percentage of the total for persons employed and for turnover for each category. Draw some conclusions from your results. (Objective A3, J1)

12   Produce a tabulation showing

a gross profit to sales ratio
b rate of turnover ratio

for each category shown in Question 6 and draw some conclusions.

13   Comment on Numac Trading Company's rate of turnover and gross profit to sales ratio (year's figures are shown in Unit 7 pages 103 and 112) compared with the Census of Distribution ratios for a company employing between 20 and 99 people (figures available in table opposite).

14 Norton Retailing Co ceased trading shortly after the following Balance Sheet was prepared. Write a report suggesting reasons why. The terms of credit sales were net cash within 30 days.

```
                    NORTON RETAILING CO

    Extract from Balance Sheet as at 31 December 19-8
                         (£000)    (£000)    (£000)
   Fixed assets
   Property and plant              83.7
   Other items                     66.6
                                   ────
                                             150.3
   Current assets
   Stock                 105.2
   Debtors                88.7
                         ─────
                                   193.9
   Less Current liabilities
   Overdraft              42.9
   Creditors              94.7
   Accruals                0.2
                         ─────
                                   137.8
                                              56.1
                                             ─────
                                             206.4
                                             ═════
```

15 Using Numac's figures for sales and gross profit for the 12 months of 19−1 (see pages 103 and 112) draw a scatter diagram to determine whether there is any recognisable relationship between sales income and gross profit. (Objective B2)

Assignment 5
Chrysler United Kingdom Ltd

(To meet objectives D2, E2, F1, H1, J1, J4)

You are required to read the accompanying information and answer the questions which follow.

The American Chrysler Company entered the UK motor car industry in 1964 when it took a minority share holding in the old established 'family' company Rootes Motors Limited. By 1967 Rootes was in serious financial trouble, and Chrysler took an increasing interest, eventually changing the name from Rootes Group to Chrysler United Kingdom Limited in 1971 and taking the company over completely in 1973.

The takeover, however, did not realise all that had been hoped. Losses of more than £35 million were incurred in the years 1965 to 1974, which included losses of more than £10 million in each of the years 1967, 1970 and 1974. When it became clear that significant losses would be incurred in 1975, without the probability of significant profits in later years, Chrysler Corporation decided that it could not continue operations in the United Kingdom.

Negotiations with the government resulted in a rescue plan. This involved massive financial aid from the government in the form of loans and grants and required Chrysler Corporation to write off loans to the UK company amounting to some £20 million, together with further loans to be made in 1976 and 1977 of £12 million for new equipment. The agreement also required the equal sharing of profits and losses in 1977, 1978 and 1979.

However, during 1978 negotiations were opened with the PSA Peugeot-Citroën car firm in France. As a result, Chrysler United Kingdom Limited was sold to the French company (along with other

Chrysler interests in Europe) for £118 million cash and £103 million of Peugeot shares. By this deal, Chrysler brought to an end its direct involvement in the European car industry; it also helped to make the Chrysler-Peugeot-Citroën Company the largest in the world, after General Motors, Ford of America and Toyota and Datsun of Japan.

This assignment is based upon Chrysler United Kingdom Ltd's reports for 1975, 1976 and 1977. The accounts have been simplified to meet the needs of students who have no knowledge of company accounts.

Chrysler United Kingdom Ltd depreciation policy

Property, plant and equipment is stated at cost, and depreciation is calculated on a straight line basis as follows:

Freehold property	—land: not provided
	—buildings: $2^{1}/_{2}\%$ of cost
	—equipment and improvements: 5% and 10% of cost
Leasehold property	—depreciated over the period of the lease
Machinery, equipment and fixtures	—depreciated over the estimated useful life of the assets. Rates vary between 4% and 16% per annum

Table 1   CHRYSLER UNITED KINGDOM LTD

Balance Sheets (simplified)
(£000)

	1974	1975	1976	1977
Fixed assets				
Property and plant	33 141	29 699	34 610	39 454
Special tools	6 777	6 757	8 938	13 954
Investments	1 296	1 623	1 623	1 623
	41 214	38 079	45 171	55 031
Current assets				
Stocks	93 635	90 794	112 760	133 906
Debtors and prepayments	30 517	25 111	25 992	43 946
Bank and cash	2 509	2 892	10 512	3 002
	126 661	118 797	149 264	180 854
	167 875	156 876	194 435	235 885
Capital	47 632	47 632	73 352	80 853
Less Accumulated loss	22 308	57 827	59 217	70 754
	25 324	(10 195)	14 135	10 099
Long term loans	26 442	33 135	62 409	83 279
	51 766	22 940	76 544	93 378
Current liabilities				
Bank loans and overdrafts	33 527	38 114	17 503	14 206
Short term loans	9 000	13 169	6 700	14 500
Creditors and accruals	73 582	82 653	93 688	113 801
	116 109	133 936	117 891	142 507
	167 875	156 876	194 435	235 885

Table 2

CHRYSLER UNITED KINGDOM LTD

Financial statistics 1971-77 (£000)

	1971	1972	1973	1974	1975	1976	1977
Sales	320 000	281 000	322 000	313 000	351 000	332 000	458 000
Net earnings (loss)	514	1 600	3 750	(17 734)	(35 519)	(42 891)	(21 537)
Depreciation:							
Property & plant	6 851	4 971	5 187	4 176	3 502	3 338	3 489
Special tools	1 401	1 480	1 960	1 719	1 796	2 979	4 270

FINANCIAL POSITION: YEAR END

	1971	1972	1973	1974	1975	1976	1977
Capital employed							
Gross fixed capital	82 498	84 691	88 732	88 322	87 823	97 150	106 098
Less Depreciation	34 201	38 864	43 766	47 108	49 744	51 979	51 067
Net fixed capital	48 297	45 827	44 966	41 214	38 079	45 171	55 031
Net current assets	18 252	20 618	14 548	10 552	(15 139)	31 373	38 347
Total capital employed	66 549	66 445	59 514	51 766	22 940	76 544	93 378

Table 3 Employees' remuneration

Year	Employees	Total wage bill
1975	28 423	£80.72m
1976	20 596	£72.34m
1977	22 800	£89.65m

Table 4 Employees earning over
£10 000 per annum

Year	10 000–12 500	12 500–15 000	15 000–17 500	Average earnings
1974	7	1	1	12 083
1975	11	4	0	11 916
1976	15	6	2	12 336
1977	25	4	5	12 279

Table 5   Index of retail prices

1969	1970	1971	1972	1973	1974	1975	1976	1977	1978
100	105	114	123	132	147	176	206	239	261

Questions

1 Calculate for the years 1974, 1975, 1976 and 1977 the following ratios:
a working capital   *c* liquidity ratio
b quick asset ratio   *d* liquidity of debtors

2 Explain how Chrysler United Kingdom Ltd have money in the bank and overdrafts appearing on the same Balance Sheet.

3 Why do you think the company does not charge depreciation on land?

4 Why does the firm use differing rates of depreciation for different types of assets?

5 Calculate the average earnings per employee for the years 1975, 1976 and 1977. Compare the percentage increase of earnings for Chrysler United Kingdom Ltd with the Index of Retail Prices.

6 Table 4 gives details of employees who earned over £10000 for the years 1975, 1976 and 1977. Would it be correct to argue that the higher paid executives, in fact, received very little increase in salary over the four years? Give reasons for your answer.

7 Compare the sales income for 1971 to 1977 inclusive with the Index of Retail Prices. Show this comparison on a semi-logarithmic scale graph.

8 During 1976 and 1977 the British government made grants to the company of £41.5 million and £10.0 million respectively. Why might a government make grants instead of loans?

9 Convert net earnings for the years 1971 to 1977, to 1971 monetary values.

10 Write a report on Chrysler United Kingdom Ltd for the years 1975, 1976 and 1977 based upon the information supplied and your own calculations.

17 Collection of business data

The activity known as book-keeping is largely one of gathering information and recording it. Throughout the course so far you have been developing a manual system of accounting: entries have been written by hand into the various accounts, and up until about 70 years ago, all firms used this manual system. Armies of clerks were employed to record the day-to-day activities of commerce and industry. Sitting on high chairs, making entries in large, leather-bound books, the main quality required of such a clerk was that he was able to write in a close, round hand and add a column of figures quickly and accurately.

A number of developments altered this picture: the advent of the typewriter, the introduction of carbon paper, the arrival of the calculating machine, the use of punch cards for commercial activities and most recently, the extensive use of computers.

The typewriter

The idea of a writing machine dates back to 1714 when Henry Mill received a patent for his method of 'impressing or transcribing letters'. Almost nothing is known of this machine, and it was in the third quarter of the nineteenth century that the modern typewriter began to emerge.

The first typewriter worthy of the name appeared in 1878, when Remington produced their Model No 2 in America. Earlier models had appeared in 1829 and 1871, with Remington's first machine being marketed in 1872, but the early machines were capable of only a limited range of work. The 1878 model was the first to write both capital and small letters.

After this, various improvements by different manufacturers led to more and more businesses adopting typewriters. In 1900, the Underwood Model No 5 introduced the front or upward stroke, an innovation which other makers were quick to follow. During the first two decades of the present century, general design became more standardised, and the machine took on the shape it has today. A successful electric typewriter was developed in 1920, but such machines were not generally introduced until the 1930's.

With the introduction of the typewriter, the masses of largely male clerks recording the activities of firms with pen and ink gave way to girls operating the new machines. The typewriter produced a neater, standardised piece of work at a lower cost.

Clearly, with the introduction of typewriters, the weighty ledgers which had been used hitherto had to change. Initially, loose-bound ledgers were used. Pages from these books were detached so that the necessary entries could be made, and the pages were then returned to the books.

It was not long before it was realised that such large ledgers were not necessary at all, and that the continual extraction and insertion of the ledger pages was a waste of time. Thin paper sheets soon tore with the constant handling, so cards were introduced. It was found that these served just as well and would wear better, provided they could be stored together and not mislaid. By using loose cards, a great deal of time could be saved.

Carbon paper

In the quill-and-ink days, the only way to obtain a copy of a letter or an account, was to write it out a second or third time. When carbon paper was introduced at the beginning of the twentieth century, the potential savings in time were enormous. In addition, a carbon copy was made at the same time as the original, so that the risk of copying errors was eliminated.

The introduction of typewriters led to special carbons being produced for the new machines, since the mechanical operation of writing with a typewriter is very different from writing with a pen or pencil. Specially produced carbon paper for typewriters was essential.

The marrying of typewriters and carbon paper opened up vast new opportunities for accounting and office work generally. Four or five copies could be produced simultaneously, and the time wasted on transcription, eliminated. Sets of documents were soon adapted whereby a number of secondary records could be produced simultaneously with the original. Hence, an invoice set might comprise:

1   the invoice, to be sent to the customer
2   a copy invoice to be kept by the firm, and from which the Sales Book would be entered. Indeed, Sales Books might be discontinued, and batches of copy invoices, bound in chronological order, used instead
3   an advice note, to be sent with the goods
4   a packing label
5   despatch authorisation, to be sent to the stores as an instruction to send off the goods

Thus, by typing the invoice, the other four documents could be produced at the same time.

Great savings could therefore be made if documents were designed specifically for use in sets. Some form of colour coding might also be employed. The opportunities presented by such multi-copy stationery interleaved with carbon paper, were legion. This was especially true when such stationery was used in 'continuous packs' so that the sets were fed into the typewriter continuously from a prepared pack.

In recent years carbon paper has been displaced by NCR (no carbon required) paper. With NCR paper, the underside of the top sheet, and the upper side of the bottom sheet are chemically treated so that when the top copy is written on, a copy is automatically produced by the interaction of the chemicals. Such papers not only produce cleaner copies but they save having to use extra carbon sheets in document sets. Using NCR paper also saves time.

Accounting machines

The accounting machine emerged from the development of the typewriter. When the typewriter was fitted with adding registers it could be made to add the figures being typed. Where ledgers and other accounting records were to be kept by such machines, they had to be of a loose-leaf form. In fact, they were generally kept on cards, with the debtors' cards being kept in one set of trays and the creditors' cards being kept in another. To ensure that the cards were not confused, they were often colour coded — yellow for debtors and green for creditors, for instance.

The cards were usually ruled in three columns, similar to the bank statements referred to in Unit 12. At the end of the accounting period, when the cards were balanced and the final accounts prepared, the cards were often bound for safe storage.

By combining different designs of stationery and carbon or NCR papers, several accounting records could be entered at the same time, with total figures and balances calculated automatically by the machine.

Punched card machines

The idea of recording information in the form of holes punched into card or paper was developed during the nineteenth century. Jacquard used a perforated card to control the patterns produced by his silk weaving machines in 1801, and in the 1830's, ships' biscuits were made by machines controlled by punched cards.

However, it was not until the end of the nineteenth century that it was realised that punched cards could be used for recording business information. The first major use of punched cards for data analysis was by Herman Hollerith in the United States census of 1880. Hollerith realised that the holes in the cards could be used to generate electrical impulses and that such a system could be used for completing the census.

Having gone through a number of changes, the most widely used form of card nowadays has 80 columns and 12 rows giving 960 punching positions. Each of these positions is given a significance by the use of a code. Thus, information to be punched into the card must first be coded so that the machines can handle it.

There are three basic stages in any punched card system:

1   the information must be punched onto the cards
2   the cards must be sorted into a desired order
3   the information on the cards must be printed back into words or figures, a process known as tabulation.

In order to perform these activities, a punched card unit will comprise three machines: a punch, a sorter and a tabulator.

When a punched card unit is used for processing accounting information, it greatly speeds the recording activity, since it is generally necessary to produce only one original recording of the information. Once a piece of accounting information is punched onto a card, that card can be manipulated at high speed by machines so that the information can be combined with that contained on other cards in numerous variations.

Hence, details from invoices sent by suppliers may be punched onto a set of cards. Once punched, the cards will be verified by a second operator to ensure that the holes have been punched in the proper places.

Next, the cards will be arranged in a desired order from which the accounting records can be produced. This arranging of the cards is performed by a sorter which processes the cards at high speed, sensing the holes in the cards, and dropping the cards into a series of boxes or pockets in the predetermined sequence. The cards might be sorted into alphabetical order, geographical order, or account number order.

The cards are then stored in trays until such time as the information on them is required. By combining the information concerning suppliers' invoices with cards showing who the firm has paid, how much, what returns have been made and what discounts taken, it is possible to have the tabulator print out the current situation of each supplier's account. By incorporating carbon interleaved or NCR stationery, the tabulator can be used to produce the firm's own printed record of its suppliers' accounts and such other monthly statements as are desired. The balance on each supplier's account can then be punched onto a set of balance cards ready for the following period's activities.

When a punched card system is used for recording accounting activities, the ledgers and day books become simply a pack of punched cards. These packs will be kept in trays to provide all the information which manually produced accounts can provide, and much, much more, since the cards can be combined in any desired mix. The basic principles of double entry accounting, however, still apply.

Computers

There are basically two types of computer: the analogue computer and the digital computer. The **analogue computer** tends to be used in process industries where it is employed to control furnace temperatures and the operation of machinery. The strength of the input signal is measured by the computer, and is used as the basis for some form of action.

A **digital computer** operates with precise numbers which it measures not by the strength of the electrical signal, but by the presence or absence of a signal. In the processing of business information, a digital computer is used.

The recognised father of the computer is Charles Babbage who in the early and mid-nineteenth century endeavoured to build a machine capable of performing a predetermined series of calculations. However, it was many years before the technical problems associated with the building of his machine could be overcome, although many of Babbage's ideas have been incorporated into modern computers.

In the early 1940's, Harvard University in America began to combine Babbage's ideas with the knowledge that had been gained from punched card machines. From this happy combination emerged the first electronic computer in 1944.

In the following years, transistors took over from valves, only to be superseded by micro integrated circuits. Developments in technology have brought about major improvements in the computer's capabilities. Now, machines can complete over a thousand calculations every second, whereas the first computer took 10 seconds to do one division calculation.

During the 1950's, computers invaded the business world, taking over much of the recording and calculating work previously performed manually or by punched card units. Clearly, a computer is an expensive machine, and its use, initially, was confined to the larger firms. However, the introduction of computer terminals where an operator can use the GPO telephone line as a link to a computer and share the computer capability with a number of other users, and smaller, desk-top models have extended the computer's use to quite small organisations.

The computer receives its input of information in coded form on punched card, punched paper tape, magnetic tape, or directly from a keyboard. In whatever manner the input is received, it is transformed into a series of electrical impulses. These impulses are passed to a storage unit to await further action.

Information within a computer can be stored in a quick access store which keeps the information available for immediate use, or in a back-up store which allows information to be stored for any period of time. Access to the back-up store is slower.

Information is brought from the store to the arithmetic unit where the necessary calculations are performed or comparisons of numbers made. The resulting information can then be returned to store, or it can be transferred to an output unit where it is taken off the computer in the form of punched cards, punched tape, or magnetic tape (which is like a spool from a tape recorder). Alternatively, it can be printed in words and numbers as a print-out.

A computer is a machine. It must be told what to do every step of the way. The nature and sequence of these instructions is called a **programme**. Once a programme has been devised, it can be put onto an input device – for example, magnetic tape – and 'run' whenever it is required. Thus, the computer can be asked to perform standard procedures at any time, no matter how complicated these procedures are.

In order to use the computer, information and instructions must be coded in a form which the computer will understand. The need for such coding quickly led to the development of common 'languages' which those responsible for using computers could readily adopt. A number of such languages are now used: Cobol (common business orientated language), Fortran (formula translation), Algol (algorithm language) and more recently, Basic (beginners all-purpose symbolic instruction code) and PL1 (programme language 1). Each was designed with certain activities in mind as suggested by their names.

These languages have a certain standardisation accepted throughout the world, and each differs from another in the same way that a language will differ by the dialects used.

A computer can do more than simply record activities, however. It can be programmed to control events. If a customer has been given a credit limit of £500, the computer can be programmed to check that this limit is not breached, and it can check this every time it makes an entry in that customer's account. The computer can also resolve complex arithmetical problems to help managers take decisions. It can be programmed to simulate activities, so that managers can ask the question 'What happens if . . .' and can see the likely results of various courses of action.

In accounting, the computer makes the recording and analysis of data simpler. It eases the conversion of data into information, but the basic double entry ideas still apply. The ledger simply becomes not a book, but a spool of tape, and the amount is represented by a number of electrical impulses passing along a circuit, rather than by a figure recorded in ink.

Summary

On completion of this unit you should be able to:

1 Describe the technological changes affecting the collection and presentation of business and financial information. (E1)

Appendix A

Commercial documents

The buying and selling of goods and services can, at its simplest level, be the exchange of cash for goods or a service. At its most complex, it is a business transaction with contractual and thus legal responsibilities. To ensure that there is no misunderstanding between the seller and buyer, the terms of the sale, the authority for purchase and the request for payment are put in writing. These documents also facilitate the maintenance of accurate accounts.

A buyer interested in obtaining a particular item or service will write to a number of suppliers to seek details of their products, price, delivery dates, specification. This is often referred to as an **enquiry**. The replies to these enquiries will be **quotations**. These are formal statements, either in a letter or a pre-printed form, giving details of the product or service, price, discounts, delivery dates and any special constraints.

The buyer will assess the various quotations received and will place an **order** with one company. The buyer will sign this on behalf of the company and this is the authority for the seller to supply to the buyer. In placing the order, the buyer infers his readiness to pay for the goods when requested to do so. An example of an order is given on page 265. Note that the form bears a serial number to ensure that a control is maintained on the issue of orders. This serial number becomes a reference number which will link any further documents issued in connection with the supply of this particular item(s).

Once the item is ready for despatch, an **advice/consignment note** is prepared (see page 266). One copy is sent by post to the customer, another is packed with the goods and another is often given to the carrier so that a receipt can be obtained showing that goods have been received. Note that it is common practice to omit prices and financial calculations from the advice/consignment note.

Once the goods have been despatched an **invoice** is prepared by the accounts department (see page 267). This is a clear statement of the goods supplied and how much is owed by the buyer.

A **statement** (see page 268) is prepared, usually at monthly intervals, listing the invoices forwarded during the last few weeks or so, and detailing any money received. It will therefore start with an outstanding balance, if there is one, and finish with the balance now due from the buyer.

If any of the goods supplied have to be returned to the seller, it is usual practice to issue a **credit note**. This is printed in red and shows details of the sum of money to be credited to the buyer which will therefore be deducted from the outstanding balance (see page 269).

On the other hand, if it is subsequently found that more goods were sent than were invoiced, or that the invoice understated the correct amount, a **debit note** will be prepared. It is similar to a credit note but is printed in black. The appropriate sum will be debited to the buyer's account and added to the outstanding balance. The debit note is simply an additional invoice which puts right an understatement of the amount due.

ORDER

Tel. No: 664422
VAT No: 147 6307 23

Messrs. R.D. JONES & CO.,
49 Kingston Road,
Northampton.

Order No: SB/107   Date: 3.1.19-1

Numac Trading Company
Norton Estate
Nottingham

Dear Sirs

    Please supply the following goods:

10 Towels, bath Ref. No. 9747 Price £8.70 each

10 Pairs single sheets,cotton Ref. No. 6921
                        Price £14.50 per pair

    This confirms our telephone enquiry today.
Delivery to be made to the above address.

                Yours faithfully,

                  R D Jones & Co

                R C Thomas

                R C Thomas
                Buyer

ADVICE/CONSIGNMENT NOTE

NUMAC TRADING COMPANY
Norton Estate
Nottingham

Telephone: 37621
Telex: 44-4343
Telegrams: Notmac

Advice Note No: 607/1

DELIVERY ADDRESS:	INVOICE ADDRESS:
Messrs R D Jones & Co 49 Kingston Road Northampton	Same

YOUR ORDER NO: SB/107	DATE OF DESPATCH: 20.1.19-1	By road

REF. NO.	DESCRIPTION	QTY.	DESPATCH DETAILS
9747	Towel, bath	10	The goods detailed have been despatched by road carrier. If the goods are not received within 7 days from date of despatch, please contact the Sales Office.
6921	Sheets, cotton, single	10	

PACKAGING DETAILS: 4 parcels

INVOICE

NUMAC TRADING COMPANY
Norton Estate
Nottingham

Telephone: 37621
Telex: 44-4343
Telegrams: Notmac

Invoice No: 3613
VAT No: 147 9898 21
Date: 23.1.19-1

Messrs R D Jones & Co
49 Kingston Road
Northampton

YOUR ORDER: SB/107				DATE OF DESPATCH: 20.1.19-1	
REF. NO.	DESCRIPTION	QTY.	UNIT PRICE	£	V.A.T. £
9747	Towel, bath	10	£ 8.70	87.00	
6921	Sheets, cotton, single	10	£14.50	145.00	
				232.00	
	VAT at 8%			18.56	18.56
				£ 250.56	

DELIVERY ADDRESS:

As above

PAYMENT DUE 30 DAYS NET.

STATEMENT

NUMAC TRADING COMPANY
Norton Estate
Nottingham

Telephone: 37621
Telex: 44-4343
Telegrams: Notmac

Date: 16.2.19-1

Messrs R D Jones & Co
49 Kingston Road
Northampton

DATE	REFERENCE	TOTAL VALUE	PAYMENTS, CREDITS	BALANCE
19-1				
23.1.	3613	£ 250.56		£ 250.56
12.2.	Cr.Note 18		£ 18.79	£ 231.77

PLEASE RETURN THIS STATEMENT WITH YOUR REMITTANCE.

CREDIT NOTE

NUMAC TRADING COMPANY
Norton Estate
Nottingham

Telephone: 37621
Telex: 44-4343
Telegrams: Notmac

Credit Note No.　18
VAT No: 147 9898 21
Date:　　12.2.19-1

Messrs R D Jones & Co
49 Kingston Road
Northampton

YOUR REF.	SB/107	OUR INVOICE	3613			
REF. NO.	DESCRIPTION		QTY.	UNIT PRICE	£	V.A.T. £
9747	Towel, bath		2	8.70	17.40	
	VAT 8%				1.39	1.39
					£ 18.79	

Goods damaged in transit and returned on 10.2.19-1.

THE ABOVE AMOUNT WILL BE CREDITED TO YOUR ACCOUNT.

Appendix B

More on pie charts, powers and roots

There will be occasions when a decision is made to present two sets
of data for comparison as pie charts with the areas of the circles
proportionate to each absolute total value. You may be given the
following information to work on:

	19-0	19-1
NUMAC TRADING CO		
Sales (£)		
Total sales	573 000	729 400
Departmental sales		
Textiles	160 000	160 000
Clothing	174 000	218 820
Furniture	150 000	261 580
Miscellaneous	89 000	89 000

The two areas of the circles for 19−0 and 19−1 must be proportionate to each other. If 4 cm is taken as the radius for circle 19−0,
the radius of circle 19−1 can be found.

Since the radius of a circle is πr^2, the radius (R) of the 19−1 circle
will be in proportion to the radius for the 19−0 circle, i.e.

573 000 : 729 400, which will be the same as $4^2 : R^2$

Thus, in our example:

$$\pi r^2 = 573\ 000 : 729\ 400\ \pi R^2 \text{ or}$$

$$\pi r^2 = \frac{573\ 000}{729\ 400} \pi R^2$$

Since the radius of the 19−0 circle is 4 cm, the equation is:

$$\pi 4^2 = \frac{573\ 000}{729\ 400} \pi R^2$$

Both sides are then divided by π to remove π from the calculation. Thus:

$$4^2 = \frac{573\ 000}{729\ 400} R^2 \text{ or } \frac{573\ 000}{729\ 400} R^2 = 4^2$$

Then multiply both sides by 729 400 to remove the divisor. Thus:

$$573\ 000\ R^2 = 4^2 \times 729\ 400$$

Then divide both sides by 573 000 to leave R^2 on its own:

$$R^2 = 4^2 \times \frac{729\ 400}{573\ 000}$$
$$R^2 = 20.36$$

Then take the square root of both sides to find R:

$$R = \sqrt{20.36}$$
$$R = 4.513\ cm$$

The radius of circle 19−1 is 4.5 cm
   The two circles can now be drawn. It is now necessary to calculate the subdivisions. The subdivisions for 19−0 are:

$$\text{Textiles} = \frac{160\ 000}{573\ 000} \times 360° = 101° \quad \text{Clothing} = \frac{174\ 000}{573\ 000} \times 360° = 109°$$

$$\text{Furniture} = \frac{150\ 000}{573\ 000} \times 360° = 94° \quad \text{Misc.} = \frac{89\ 000}{573\ 000} \times 360° = 56°$$

(See page 272)

272

NUMAC TRADING CO
sales 19-0

FURNITURE

MISCELLANEOUS

TEXTILES

CLOTHING

NUMAC TRADING CO
sales 19-1

FURNITURE

MISCELLANEOUS

CLOTHING

TEXTILES

Using this same method, the degrees of the circle for each subdivision for 19−1 are: Textiles 79°, Clothing 108°, Furniture 129° and Miscellaneous 44°. (See page 272)

Be warned that pie charts can be misleading. From the pie charts on page 272 it would appear that sales of Textiles and Miscellaneous have dropped. They have not dropped in absolute terms, but in proportion to total sales, they have.

The Electricity Council handbook of Electricity Supply Statistics 1977 uses pie diagrams to show the change in expenditure from 1972/3 to 1976/7. The areas have been drawn in proportion to total expenditure:

ANALYSIS OF ELECTRICITY REVENUE ACCOUNT EXPENDITURE 1972/73 & 1976/77

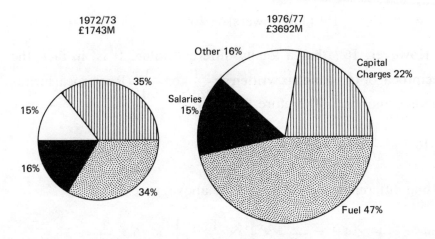

Reference has been made above to r^2 or a number squared. To develop this idea further, it can be seen that:

$4^2 = 4^1 \times 4^1 = 16$ (Note that the power sign has been added). Thus: $4^2 \times 4^2 = 4^4$ (i.e. when multiplying two figures, you add their powers)

The opposite procedure is to take a square root. Thus:

$$\sqrt{4} = \sqrt{2 \times 2} = 2 \text{ or } \sqrt{16} = \sqrt{4 \times 4} = 4$$

However, $\sqrt{16}$ can also be shown as $16^{1/2}$. This can be proved by multiplying $\sqrt{16}$ by $\sqrt{16}$ which is $4 \times 4 = 16$. Or, using powers:

$16^{1/2} \times 16^{1/2} = 16^1$ (add powers) $= 16$

However, $16^{-1/2}$ has a totally different value. It is, in fact, the reciprocal of $16^{1/2}$ which is written as $\dfrac{1}{16^{1/2}}$ or $\dfrac{1}{\sqrt{16}}$ (Reciprocal means 1 over a number). Therefore:

16^{-1} is $\dfrac{1}{16}$ and 16^{-2} is $\dfrac{1}{16^2}$

Using different values to prove the above,

$$4^{-1/2} \times 4^2 \times 4^{-1} = \frac{1}{\sqrt{4}} \times 4^2 \times \frac{1}{4} = \frac{1}{2} \times 16 \times \frac{1}{4} = 2$$
$$\text{or } 4^{-1/2} \times 4^2 \times 4^{-1} = 4^{-1/2+2-1} = 4^{1/2} = \sqrt{4} = 2$$

Making the problem a little more complex you should see that $16^{1/4}$ can be interpreted as

$$\sqrt[4]{16^3} = \sqrt[4]{(2 \times 2 \times 2 \times 2)^3} = 2^3 = 8$$

and that $16^{-3/4}$ can be interpreted as $\dfrac{1}{\sqrt[4]{16^3}} = \dfrac{1}{8}$

Note that all the above comments refer to situations when multiplying and dividing numbers with powers. It will not work when adding or subtracting numbers with powers. Thus: $2^2 \times 2^2$ is not the same as $2^2 + 2^2$.

The principles have been established above using small numbers, but in a practical situation the numbers will be larger and more difficult to handle. If a calculator is not available use logarithms, remembering that:

$16^{3/4} = \sqrt[4]{16^3}$. Thus, the logarithm will be:

$$\frac{\log 16}{4} \times 3$$

As we have proved above, the answer should be 8.

log 16 is 1.2041
$1.2041 \div 4 = 0.3010$: $0.3010 \times 3 = 0.9030$
anti-log $= 7.998$
Rounded to nearest integer $= 8$

Summary

On completion of this Appendix plus practice at the exercises you should be able to:

1 Construct a pie chart where the areas are required to be proportional to the totals.
2 Calculate and manipulate roots and powers. (A4)

Exercises

1 Using the information supplied in the pie diagrams on page 273, calculate the absolute values for the four categories for each year. Tabulate this information with the relative figures. Present the information using another diagrammatic form which you consider effectively highlights the changes over the 5 years. (Objective C2)

2 Using the information given below, construct pie charts for 1972 and 1976 in proportion to their totals.

Total UK Premiums (Insurance)

	1972 £m	1976 £m
Liability	109	267
Motor	382	743
Pecuniary loss	72	147
Personal accident	28	57
Property	327	674
Total	918	1888

(Objectives A4, C2)

3 Evaluate:

a $x^{-2} \times x^{-1/4} \times x^3$

b $y^3 \times y^2 \times y^3$

c $x^{-1/2} \times x^{-1/2} \times x^{-1/2}$

d $c^3 \times c^2 \times c^{-1/2}$

e $f^4 \times f^{-1/4} \times f^{1/4}$

f $\dfrac{n^3 \times n^2}{n^4}$

g $\dfrac{n^5 \times n^3}{n^{1/2} \times n^{1/2}}$

h $\dfrac{\sqrt[3]{n^2 \times n^3}}{\sqrt{n}}$

(Objective A4)

Appendix C

Logarithms of numbers less than one. More on depreciation.

For whole numbers it is very easy to calculate a characteristic and then look up the mantissa. But what happens with a number less than 1?

log 1000 = 3
log 100 = 2
log   10 = 1
log   0 = 0
log   0.1 = ?

Looking at the characteristics, a pattern is emerging: 3, 2, 1, 0. What comes next? Minus one, so the characteristic of log 0.1 is -1. The characteristic of log 0.01 is -2 and so on. Since it is only the characteristic which is negative, the minus sign is put above the figure: $\bar{1}, \bar{2}$ and it is called bar 1, bar 2.

In Unit 7 the log of 77 was found. This was 1.8865. The log of 0.77 is $\bar{1}$.8865. How can you perform a calculation using the logs of numbers less than one? Suppose you wish to calculate 0.35×0.26:

no	log
0.35	$\bar{1}$.5441
0.26	$\bar{1}$.4150
(add)	$\bar{2}$.9591
anti-log =	9.101

As usual, the decimal point is put after the first digit of the anti-log. Then look at the characteristic to see how many places to move it. The bar indicates that it must be moved to the left, 2 places. Thus $0.35 \times 0.26 = .09101$

You may not always begin with a bar figure. Suppose you wish to calculate $12 \div 37$

no	log
12	1.0792
37	1.5682

Unfortunately, the log of 37 is greater than the log of 12. The mantissa must remain a positive number, so 1 is added to both parts of the sum:

no	log
12	1.$^{1+}$0792
37	1+1. 5682

It is now possible to subtract the mantissas, but for the characteristics the sum is now $1-2$, which gives an answer of minus 1. However, we know this is possible since decimal fractions have negative characteristics.

no	log
12	1.0792
37	1.5682

(subtract) $\bar{1}.5110$ ($\bar{1}$ tells us to move the decimal point one place to the left.)

anti-log $= 3.243$

$12 \div 37 = 0.3243$

Where there is a need to take a root of a number, it is simply done by finding the log of the number, dividing that log by its root and then obtaining the anti-log. For example:

$^5\sqrt{0.0085}$

The logarithm is $\bar{3}.9294$. In dividing this by 5, the $\bar{3}$ must not be mixed with the positive mantissa of .3929. We therefore perform a balancing act of making $\bar{3}$ into $\bar{5}$ so that the division will be a whole number. To make $\bar{3}$ into $\bar{5}$ we have to add $\bar{2}$ to $\bar{3}$. This is balanced by giving $+2$ to the mantissa. Thus we have $\bar{5}$ and 2.9294.

Dividing these two by 5 gives us $\bar{1}$ and .5858. We then put these together to get $\bar{1}.5858$. The anti-log is 0.3853. Thus the $\sqrt[5]{0.0085}$ is 0.3853.

A knowledge of logs of numbers less than one can help when working out some of the more difficult depreciation equations. Unit 15 explained the straight line method of depreciation. Another method is to apply a fixed percentage depreciation to the balance of an asset's value.

To find the percentage, the following formula is used.

$$r = 1 - \sqrt[n]{\frac{s}{c}}$$

where n = number of years

s = the net residual value

c = the cost of the asset and

r = the rate of depreciation to be applied.

Using the figures on page 214, a new lathe costs £8500 with a useful life of 5 years and a scrap (residual) value of £500. Using the formula,

$$r = 1 - \sqrt[5]{\frac{500}{8500}}$$

the value for r, the rate of depreciation, can be found. This is probably best worked out using logarithms, since a 1/5th root cannot be calculated using a simple electronic calculator.

log	500	2.6990
log	8500	3.9294
		$\overline{2}.7696$
(divide by 5)		$\bar{1}.7539$
anti-log =		0.5674

$r = 1 - 0.5674 = 0.4326$ (or 43%)

Proof   8500
Yr 1 Depreciation 43.26% of 8500 = 3677
                                                     ─────
                                                       4823
Yr 2 Depreciation 43.26% of 4823 = 2086
                                                     ─────
                                                       2737
Yr 3 Depreciation 43.26% of 2737 = 1184
                                                     ─────
                                                       1553
Yr 4 Depreciation 43.26% of 1553 = 672
                                                     ─────
                                                        881
Yr 5 Depreciation 43.26% of 881 =   381
                                                     ─────
                                                     £500

This method provides the same residual value for the lathe, but the actual value and depreciation are different each year.

Summary

On completion of this Appendix plus practice at the exercises you should be able to:

1 Calculate depreciation by the reducing balance method.
2 Calculate powers and roots where logarithms are required.

Exercises

1 Calculate the following by use of logarithms:

$a \quad \sqrt[3]{\dfrac{512.76}{746.3}}$
$b \quad \sqrt[5]{\dfrac{842 \times 730}{1263}}$
$c \quad \sqrt[4]{\dfrac{967}{82 \times 47}}$

$d \quad 1 - \sqrt[3]{\dfrac{270}{640}}$
$e \quad \sqrt[6]{\dfrac{94\,762}{7537}}$
$f \quad \sqrt[4]{\dfrac{83\,723}{84\,760}}$

(Objective A4)

2 A machine is purchased for £50 000 with an expected life of 5 years and a residual value of £3000. Calculate by the reducing balance method the percentage depreciation to be applied each year. Check your answer by showing the actual amounts depreciated each year. (Objective A4)

3 A piece of office equipment is purchased for £5000 with an expected life of 10 years and a residual value of £200. Calculate by the reducing balance method the percentage depreciation to be applied each year. Check your answer by showing the actual amount of depreciation for each year. (Objective A4)

4 Using the two examples given in Unit 15 and Appendix C, compare the two methods of applying depreciation. What are the advantages of each method? Are there any disadvantages?

0282

Appendix D

Value Added Tax

Value Added Tax – usually abbreviated to VAT – was introduced
into Britain on 1 April 1974. Its introduction was made necessary
when Britain joined the Common Market: the Treaty of Rome,
under which the European Economic Community is established,
provided that a system of taxation based upon value added should be
introduced by all member countries. When Britain joined the EEC,
therefore, VAT had to be introduced to conform with the Treaty
provisions.

Value added

A tax on value added is not a tax on profit. It is a tax on the increase
in the value of goods or a service which comes about as a result of a
firm's operations. For instance, a firm may purchase raw materials
for £500, perform some operation on these materials, and sell the
finished items for £1200. The value added by the firm is £1200 – £500
i.e. £700. Note that no mention has been made of profit. (In order to
calculate profit, numerous expenses must be allowed for, as in a
normal Profit and Loss Account. These expenses are not included
when calculating value added.) **VAT** *taxes added value*; it does not
tax profit.

However, the system used does not require the actual amount of
added value to be calculated in order to calculate the tax. The
desired figure is reached in another way.

The tax

VAT is collected by the Customs and Excise, and not the Inland
Revenue. Businesses with more than the minimum annual turnover
laid down in the regulations – and this minimum may change from

time to time — must register with the Customs and Excise. In return, the business is granted a VAT number against which all of its VAT activities will be conducted.

The tax is levied on the supply of goods and services throughout the United Kingdom, and upon imports into the UK. The tax is calculated at each stage of production or distribution. Thus, at each stage the taxable person — or business — is charged VAT by his suppliers on those goods or services which they supply to him. This applies not only to items bought for processing or for resale, but to capital items, too. These goods or services are flowing into the firm: they are the firm's inputs, and the tax which the firm pays on these is known as its **input tax**.

When the firm eventually supplies its own customers with goods or services — not necessarily the same ones which it received itself — the firm must charge tax to its customers. This is called the firm's **output tax**.

Every three months, when the firm makes its return to the Customs and Excise, it adds up the output tax and the input tax, and subtracts the smaller amount from the larger. If the input tax is greater than the output, then the firm can recoup the difference from the Customs and Excise. If the output tax is greater than the input tax — as is more usual — the firm must arrange to pay the difference to the Customs and Excise. This calculation of input and output tax is performed in a separate VAT Account.

The calculations

When VAT was first introduced into the United Kingdom, the standard rate was fixed at 10%. Since then it has fluctuated, but the rate of 10% will be used here in all the examples for ease of calculation.

To see how the calculation is performed, consider a customer who purchases an item from Numac Trading Co costing £200. Added to this price will be the VAT at 10%, thus the customer actually pays £220 for the article. The sequence of events, and the calculation leading up to the final sale, might be as shown on page 284.

The manufacturer purchases raw materials for £40, and pays an extra £4 for VAT at 10%. This £4 is the manufacturer's input tax, since it is paid on materials which he inputs to the final product.

	£	£	
1 *Manufacturer*			
Sum paid for raw materials	40		
VAT at 10%		4	= 4· paid to supplier
Total cost	44		
Price sold to wholesaler	100		
VAT at 10%		10	= 10 collected from wholesaler
Sale price	110	6	paid to Customs and Excise

Value added: £100 - £40 = £60 @ 10% = £6

2 *Wholesaler*			
Purchase price	100		
VAT at 10%		10	= 10 paid to manufacturer
Total cost	110		
Price sold to retailer	140		
VAT at 10%		14	= 14 collected from retailer
	154	4	paid to Customs and Excise

Value added: £140 - £100 = £40 @ 10% = £4

3 *Retailer (Numac)*			
Purchase price	140		
VAT at 10%		14	= 14 paid to wholesaler
Total cost	154		
Sold to customer	200		
VAT at 10%		20	= 20 collected from customer
	220	6	paid to Customs and Excise

Value added: £200 - £140 = £60 @ 10% = £6

4 *Final customer*			
Purchase price	200		
VAT at 10%		20	= 20 paid to retailer
Total cost	220		

Eventually, when the manufacturer has completed the work on the item, it is sold to the wholesaler for £100. However, the wholesaler must pay the VAT on top of this, so he pays a further £10. To the manufacturer, this £10 is his output tax, since it is levied on the item which he has produced and sold; in other words, his output. When the manufacturer deducts the input tax of £4 from the output tax of £10, he must pay the difference of £6 to the Customs and Excise.

In the example opposite note firstly, that the manufacturer has added value to the item equivalent to £60. The raw materials cost £40, whereas the finished item was sold for £100. The value added therefore is £100 − £40 = £60. The tax on this at 10% is £6, and this is what the manufacturer pays to the Customs and Excise.

Secondly, note that the manufacturer's output tax balances the wholesaler's input tax. The wholesaler buys the items from the manufacturer for £100 plus £10 VAT. When the wholesaler eventually sells the item to Numac − the retailer − it costs £140 plus VAT, which at 10% of £140 is £14. The wholesaler deducts *his* input tax of £10 from *his* output tax of £14, and pays the difference of £4 to the Customs and Excise. The wholesaler has added value to the item represented by the difference between his purchase price and his selling price: £140 − £100 = £40. 10% of this is £4, and this is the sum which the wholesaler pays to the Customs and Excise.

Numac, as the retailer, buys the item at £140 plus £14 VAT and sells it to the customer for £200. Numac's input tax is £14, whilst its output tax at 10% of £200 is £20. The difference of £6 is paid by Numac to the Customs and Excise. This £6 represents 10% of the value added to the item by Numac's activities, since the article was purchased for £140 and was sold for £200: £200 − £140 = £60. 10% of this is £6.

The customer thus pays £200 for the item plus £20 VAT. Since the final customer is not a taxable person registered for VAT, he cannot reclaim the VAT he has paid, neither can he pass it on. He must thus bear the whole of the tax.

By adding the separate amounts remitted to the Customs and Excise one can see how the £20 has been collected. The raw material supplier paid £4, the manufacturer £6, the wholesaler £4 and Numac £6. In total, £20 was paid. Since VAT is collected in this stage-by-stage manner, it is sometimes referred to as a cascade tax.

VAT Account

In order to keep a check on the amounts of input and output tax, each registered business – or taxable person – will keep a VAT Account. This account will record input tax on the debit side, and output tax on the credit side.

VAT Account	
Input tax	Output tax

Credit transactions

When taxable items are bought or sold on credit, the necessary entries will be made in the Purchases Book or the Sales Book in the normal way (see Unit 13). The only real difference where VAT is concerned is that the books will carry extra columns to record the VAT.

Assume that Numac purchased taxable items as follows:

Jan 8   Universal Trading Co   £340 plus VAT
14   General Supplies   £260 plus VAT
25   Commercial Appliances   £470 plus VAT

The Purchases Book would appear as shown opposite. The total in the Purchases column would be transferred to the debit side of the Purchases Account, being the total of credit purchases for January. The entries on the credit side of the individual supplier accounts would be made in the usual way, using the figures from the Total Invoice column. The total of the VAT column, representing the input tax, would be transferred to the debit side of the VAT Account.

When Numac pays its suppliers, the total amount including the tax, will be entered in the Cash Book, since this is the amount which the firm owes its suppliers. It is up to the suppliers to account for the tax element themselves, just as Numac will account for the VAT which it collects.

Purchases Book

Date		Purchases	VAT	Total
Jan 8	Universal Trading	340	34	374
14	General Supplies	260	26	286
25	Commercial Appliances	470	47	517
		1 070	107	1 177
		To Purchases Account	To VAT Account	To Supplier's Account

Universal Trading

		£
	Jan 8 Purchases	374

General Supplies

		£
	Jan 14 Purchases	286

Commercial Appliances

		£
	Jan 25 Purchases	517

Purchases

	£
Jan 31 Credit purchases for month	1 070

VAT Account

Input tax	£
Jan 31 Total for month	107

With credit sales, the situation is similar. Assume that in January, Numac made the following credit sales of taxable items:

Jan 10   C Hurne   £170 plus VAT
   15   B Blower   £210 plus VAT
   23   G Wells   £80 plus VAT
   29   W Chown £110 plus VAT

The sales appear in the Sales Book as usual. The total of the Sales column would be transferred to the credit side of the Sales Account, showing the total credit sales for January. The individual customer accounts will be debited with the full amount shown in the Total column. The total of the VAT column is then transferred to the credit side of the VAT Account.

```
                              Sales Book
      Date                    Sales      VAT        Total

      Jan 10    C Hurne        170         17         187
          15    B Blower       210         21         231
          23    G Wells         80          8          88
          29    W Chown        110         11         121
                              _____      _____      _____
                               570         57         627
                              =====      =====      =====
                                 To         To          To
                              Sales        VAT    Customer's
                              Account   Account     Account

                         C Hurne
      _____
                                 £
      Jan 10 Sales              187

                         B Blower
      _____
                                 £
      Jan 15 Sales              231

                         G Wells
      _____
                                 £
      Jan 23 Sales               88
```

W Chown				
	£			
Jan 29 Sales	121			

Sales				
				£
		Jan 31 Credit sales for month		570

VAT Account				
	£			£
Input tax Jan 31 Total for month	107	Output tax Jan 31 Total for month		57

When the debtors eventually pay Numac, the total amount received, including the tax, will be entered in the Cash Book.

Cash transactions

Where taxable items are bought or sold for cash or cheque, the amount of the tax is entered in specially ruled VAT columns in the Cash Book.

Cash Book

Disc.	VAT	Cash	Bank	Disc.	VAT	Cash	Bank

Note that the VAT columns in the Cash Book are used *only* where taxable items *which have not already passed through the Purchases or Sales Book* are bought or sold for cash or cheque. If a debtor pays his account by cheque and the sales were previously recorded in the Sales Book, no entry will be made in the VAT columns in the Cash Book. Similarly, if the firm pays a supplier by cheque, and the purchases were entered earlier in the Purchases Book, the Cash Book VAT column will not be used.

Cash Book

	Disc. £	VAT £	Cash £	Bank £		Disc. £	VAT £	Cash £	Bank £
Feb 6 C Hurne				187	Feb 7 Universal Trading				374
B Blower				271	8 Purchases		7		77
7 Sales		6	78						

Assume that on 6 February, Numac received cheques from C Hurne £187 and B Blower £271, and that on 7 February Numac paid Universal Trading the amount outstanding £374. The Cash Book would appear as shown opposite.

However, if taxable items had been sold for cash over the counter, an entry would have been made in the Cash Book's VAT columns. If cash sales on 7 February were £78, of which £6 was VAT, the entry would be made as shown opposite. Note that the tax is not deducted in the cash column as it is with cash discounts. However, the Sales Account in the above example will be credited with only £72. The total of the VAT column at the end of the week or month will be credited to the VAT Account as part of Numac's output tax.

Similarly, if on 8 February Numac purchased items for resale at £70 plus VAT, paying by cheque, the Cash Book entry would appear as shown opposite. Again, the tax is not deducted in the Cash column, although only £70 will appear on the debit side of the Purchases Account. The VAT of £7 is part of Numac's input tax for the month, and at the month-end, the total of the VAT column will be transferred to the debit side of the VAT Account.

```
                       NUMAC TRADING CO
                        VAT Account

              £       £                        £       £
Input tax                     Output tax
January     2 218             January        2 846
February    2 147             February       3 264
March       3 842             March          3 884
            ─────   8 207                    ─────   9 994
Tax payable         1 787

                    9 994                            9 994
                    ═════                            ═════
```

At the end of the quarter, the VAT Account is balanced. If the total of the output tax is greater than the total of the input tax, then the firm must pay the balance to the Customs and Excise. If, on the other hand, the input tax is greater than the output tax, the firm receives the difference from the Customs and Excise.

Above is Numac Trading Co's VAT Account for the three months ended 31 March 19–1. Since the total of the output tax £9994 is greater than the input tax £8207, Numac must pay the difference £1787 to the Customs and Excise. When payment is made, the VAT Account will be debited and the Bank Account credited.

Similarly, should money be received from Customs and Excise, the VAT Account will be credited, and the Bank Account debited.

Different rates of tax

Thus far, the discussion has assumed that there is only one rate of Value Added Tax, but there may well be two or three different rates. In such cases the VAT Account must be ruled to record separately the inputs and outputs at the different rates illustrated on page 293.

The Cash Book must also be ruled with separate columns for the different rates, but the operation of the Cash Book when there are two or more rates is similar to when there is only one.

Exempt and zero rated items

The VAT regulations designate certain goods and services as exempt from Value Added Tax. In other words, a person supplying such items or services does not have to charge VAT on them. If he deals only in such items, he does not have to register for VAT purposes, but neither can he reclaim any input tax which he might pay. If a business deals in standard rated items and exempt items it can reclaim input tax only on standard rated items: input tax on exempt items cannot be reclaimed, since they are outside VAT.

Zero rated items are technically taxable, but the rate of tax is nil. This means that VAT which a firm may be charged on inputs related to them can be reclaimed like any other input tax.

Capital items

VAT is chargeable upon many capital items which a firm may purchase. Where input tax is paid on capital items, it must be recorded in the VAT Account as normal. Such input tax will then be deducted from the output tax to reduce the firm's VAT liability.

NUMAC TRADING CO

VAT Account

Input tax	Standard rate £	Higher rate £	Total £	Output tax	Standard rate £	Higher rate £	Total £
January	1 891	327		January	2 126	720	
February	1 914	233		February	2 974	290	
March	2 947	895		March	2 839	1 045	
	6 752	1 455	8 207		7 939	2 055	
Tax payable			1 787				
			9 994				9 994
							9 994

294

Index